A BRIEF HISTORY *of*

OLD TESTAMENT CRITICISM

FROM BENEDICT SPINOZA TO BREVARD CHILDS

MARK S. GIGNILLIAT

ZONDERVAN®

ZONDERVAN

A Brief History of Old Testament Criticism
Copyright © 2012 by Mark S. Gignilliat

This title is also available as a Zondervan ebook.

Requests for information should be addressed to:
Zondervan, *Grand Rapids, Michigan 49530*

Library of Congress Cataloging-in-Publication Data

Gignilliat, Mark S.
    A brief history of Old Testament criticism : from Benedict Spinoza to Brevard Childs /
    Mark S. Gignilliat.
        p. cm.
    Includes bibliographical references and index.
    ISBN 978-0-310-32532-1 (softcover)
    1. Bible. 2. O.T.—Criticism, interpretation, etc.—History. I. Title.
BS1160.G54   2012
221.609—dc23   2011046348

Cover design: www.wdesigncompany.com
Cover art: Gustave Dore, Rembrandt van Rijn
Interior design: Beth Shagene

Printed in the United States of America

HB 09.20.2022

A Brief History *of*

Dedicated to
Michael P.V. Barrett

Μνημονεύετε τῶν ἡγουμένων ὑμῶν,
οἵτινες ἐλάλησαν ὑμῖν τὸν λόγον τοῦ θεοῦ,
ὧν ἀναθεωροῦντες τὴν ἔκβασιν
τῆς ἀναστροφῆς μιμεῖσθε τὴν πίστιν.

HEBREWS 13:7

CONTENTS

ACKNOWLEDGMENTS

ONE OF THE BLESSINGS OF ACADEMIC LIFE IS THE RICH CONVERSATIONS with colleagues and friends who like batting around ideas. I am grateful for such friends and am sure to leave out names I should have included. I should make special mention of Gerald Bray. Gerald read the manuscript and made helpful suggestions for improvement. Another friend and colleague, Ken Mathews, was kind enough to read and comment on the Albright chapter. Nathan MacDonald deserves special mention as well; he read an earlier draft of a chapter. Michael Garrett's sharp eye was a real aid toward the end of the writing phase. Jonathan Pennington and Don Collett provide a constant stream of thoughtful interaction. I am grateful for their friendship and critical engagement. My doctoral supervisor, Christopher Seitz, continues to provide an important presence in my life and work. I have learned much from conversation and simply observing his mind at work. I am grateful to all the participants of the summer writing workshop at the Center of Theological Inquiry, especially the leader of the workshop, Dr. Marilynne Robinson. I was privileged to be part of such a distinguished group and to experience the warm hospitality of CTI. My thanks go to my colleagues at Beeson Divinity School, Samford University. Around the halls of Beeson Divinity School, I benefit much from conversations with Carl Beckwith, Mark Devine, Lyle Dorsett, Allen Ross, Frank Thielman, and Doug Webster, to mention only a few of my colleagues. Betsy Childs read an earlier draft and provided needed editorial comments. My dean, Timothy George, encourages his faculty in their work and teaching. I am thankful for his support. Dr. Brad Creed, provost of Samford University, and Dr. Nancy Biggio gave me a summer research grant to attend the workshop at CTI. I am very grateful for their generosity and leadership on the campus at Samford.

The folks at Zondervan have been a delight. Katya Covrett shared the initial vision of this work and was willing to take a risk on me. She helped keep me focused even when I wanted to turn the book into something other than the original design. I am grateful for their patience and extension on a deadline (maybe two!). Bill and Martha Gignilliat, my parents, always deserve more attention and thanks than I give. I am blessed to have parents who are constantly supportive and encouraging. My wife, Naomi, and our three sons, William, Jackson, and Franklin, keep my feet planted in a world marked by love, joy, and the frenetic activity of three young sons. I can't imagine life without them. Naomi became a helpful reader toward the end of the project. I had not yet tapped into this aspect of her broad-ranging set of talents; I imagine she may regret revealing this latent skill. The book is better because of all these people and many more left unmentioned.

I am grateful for my undergraduate and seminary teachers — now more than ever. I have been blessed with many good and caring professors who have taken a special interest in my academic and spiritual growth. I am dedicating this book to one teacher in particular, Dr. Michael P.V. Barrett. It was in Dr. Barrett's Old Testament courses where as an undergrad a fire was lit in me for rigorous and thoughtful exegesis of Scripture. I have vivid memories of lecture halls filled with students, mouth agape at the clarity and profundity of Dr. Barrett's lectures. We were all scared of him. "Where did that come from, Dr. Barrett?" one of my friends shouted out in a moment of self-forgetfulness. "Well, Mr. Gage, I got it from the Bible. Do you ever read your Bible?" Though we were scared of him, we loved him and still do. I have not been very good at keeping in contact with Dr. Barrett. Intended letters are still left unwritten. I imagine he is not especially happy about all of the ecclesial and theological decisions I have made; I'm not sure I'm happy with all of them either. Nevertheless, I am grateful for the light and heat of Dr. Barrett's lectures and life. The academicians and theologians who walk the halls of an ETS, SBL, or AAR conference may never know Dr. Barrett's name. I am quite sure he does not care. But he had a shaping influence on me, and I am deeply thankful. I dedicate this book to him in grateful appreciation.

INTRODUCTION

WHEN I BEGAN MY POSTGRADUATE WORK IN BIBLICAL STUDIES, I DID SO like many who exit from an evangelical seminary. My knowledge of the biblical languages was decent. I could analyze a Hebrew sentence, parse the verbs, make sense of the syntax by appealing to Waltke and O'Connor's massive tome, and even engage the textual-critical issues involved. In retrospect, my knowledge in these areas was not as deep or wide as I might have thought at the time. Still, I had the rudimentary skills necessary for the exegesis of the biblical text, and, wisely or unwisely, they admitted me for postgraduate work.[1]

What I discovered during the first year of my doctoral studies, in addition to the imposter syndrome that haunted me, wondering when my doctoral supervisor would tap me on the shoulder and say, "I'm sorry; we've made a terrible mistake and you need to go home," was my woeful lack of knowledge in the history of Old Testament interpretation and criticism. This is not a reflection on my seminary teachers; one can only cover so much in class. We read Dillard and Longman's *Introduction to the Old Testament*. The names Wellhausen and Gunkel were not foreign to me. Still, my knowledge of these figures, their methods, and location in the history of ideas was thin at best.

I will not project my story on everybody, but I imagine my experience is common. With great interest and relief, I read Richard Schultz's account of his first years of postgraduate studies at Yale under Brevard Childs.[2] In his essay, he recounts a similar narrative: a working knowledge of lower-critical matters such as Hebrew, textual criticism, and literary analysis of

---

1. I actually did postgraduate work on Paul and Isaiah, spending equal amounts of time in New Testament and Old Testament exegesis.
2. Richard Schultz, "Brevard S. Childs's Contribution to Old Testament Interpretation: An Evangelical Appreciation and Assessment," *Princeton Theological Review* 14 (2008): 71–72.

texts and a flimsy working knowledge of higher critical figures and theories. I read his essay and thought, "Maybe I should write a short history of Old Testament criticism targeted at students." Well, here it is.

This is a book for students. A student is not limited to someone enrolled in a formal class setting, though I definitely have this in mind. Nor is this book only for those wishing to do postgraduate studies. The intended audience of this book is anyone who is interested in the Bible, its history of interpretation, and the particular problems and approaches to Old Testament studies in the modern period. I do hope the book will be of some benefit to those whose knowledge of Old Testament criticism goes beyond that of a student's. But I had to fight the temptation at every turn to allow this book to take on a life of its own, becoming something other than what was originally conceived. In places, I am sure I have failed in this regard.

A few words should be said about the scope and structure of the book — a road map, if you will, for the reader and teacher. Let me say on the front end what this book is not. This book is by no means a comprehensive attempt at expounding the very complex history of Old Testament interpretation. This kind of project is underway now with the magisterial work Magne Saebø is editing titled *Hebrew Bible/Old Testament* (HBOT).[3] The volumes in HBOT are an impressive achievement and upon completion will be the standard in the field. What Ludwig Diestel's *History of the Old Testament in the Christian Church* was for the nineteenth and early twentieth century, HBOT will be for our time.[4] All this to say, the book you are holding is a toe's dip in a very large pool.

I have decided to focus on major figures in a picture gallery tour of sorts. My rationale is simple. People and their ideas are more interesting (at least to me) than abstract discussions of critical theories. For example, I do not have a chapter on form criticism. But I do have a chapter on Hermann Gunkel, with form criticism discussed therein. Also, I find these figures fascinating as people located in the broader cross-stream of ideas, cultural norms, and ecclesiastical battles. At the same time, the context provided for these figures could surely be expanded. The chapters follow the clas-

---

3. Magne Saebø, *Hebrew Bible/Old Testament: The History of Its Interpretation* (Göttingen: Vandenhoeck & Ruprecht, 1996, 2000, 2008). A similar though not as comprehensive approach can be found in Hans-Joachim Kraus, *Geschichte der historisch-kritischen Erforschung des Alten Testaments*, 3rd ed. (Neukirchen-Vluyn: Neukirchener Verlag, 1982).

4. Ludwig Diestel, *Geschichte des Alten Testamentes in der christlichen Kirche* (Jena: Mauke's Verlag, 1869). Interestingly, HBOT is dedicated to the memory of Diestel.

sic genre of life and work. I will discuss briefly the life and setting of the figure and then explore an aspect of their contribution to Old Testament criticism.

There are dangers with the particular historiographical approach I have taken. Saebø's introductory article in HBOT labels one of these dangers "personalism," and he warns against focusing so much on "well-known scholars" that the textured nature of Old Testament interpretation will be flattened.[5] In other words, focusing solely on the famous pictures in a museum may cause the patron unwittingly to miss the multifaceted beauty and complexity of other paintings and influences from the same period of art history.

Saebø's is a fair warning, and one I take seriously. I have tried to provide some historical, social, and intellectual context for the figures described. Still, the dangers of personalism are present in this volume and can be remedied by further study for those interested. I want students to understand some of the major currents of Old Testament criticism, beginning in the modern period and continuing to the work of Brevard Childs. To do this, I have focused on particular figures. Without doubt, the chapters demand more nuance than is currently presented, but I hope the reader will take this book's stated intention into account whenever frustration occurs.

One may ask how someone can write even a brief history of Old Testament criticism and not include, say, Jean Astruc, Johann David Michaelis, Richard Simon, Johannes Semler, Robert Lowth, J. G. Eichhorn, Abraham Kuenen, Wilhelm Gesenius, Bernard Duhm, Hugo Gressmann, Walther Eichrodt, Martin Noth, or James Barr (to name but a few). I feel the full weight of this criticism and can only ask the informed reader's forgiveness. My rationale is simple: (1) I want the volume to remain small and accessible for students; (2) I believe the figures in this work represent the larger trends and tendencies of Old Testament criticism in the modern period; and (3) I wanted to finish.

As will become apparent, I am not a neutral observer of the history of Old Testament criticism. The detaching of a robust doctrine of revelation from the material study of the Old Testament, a hermeneutical instinct one finds poignantly present in Baruch Spinoza, has had a deleterious effect on the study of the Old Testament as Scripture. Here my cards are already on

---

5. Saebø, *Hebrew Bible/Old Testament*, vol. 1, part 1, 30.

the table, are they not? I do not want to make villains of the usual suspects in this volume. In fact, the reader may sense my deep sympathies for the intellectual and spiritual difficulties faced by some of these figures. Still, I have a working understanding of the Old Testament as Christian Scripture that not only informs my reading but in fact determines and shapes the way I approach it. I am not neutral. But my lack of neutrality when it comes to Old Testament hermeneutics is located in an Anselmian epistemology — *credo ut intelligam*: "I believe so that I may understand" — and a confessional posture. That said, I do hope readers find a fair presentation of these figures' lives and work. This has been my aim.

I will return to these matters in the conclusion. For now, let me introduce you to Benedict Spinoza.

BENEDICT SPINOZA

(1632–1677)

Modernity's Changing Tide and the Dislocation of Scripture from Revelation

BENEDICT DE SPINOZA IS A WATERSHED FIGURE IN THE HISTORY OF BIBLI-cal interpretation. His approach to biblical studies was not born in a vac-uum. Nor was his approach to biblical studies the first to raise critical questions about the Bible. Nevertheless, Spinoza is a significant figure because of his bold and bald articulation of the matter. Others before him had taken a critical approach to the historical character of Scripture and its claims — Thomas Hobbes and Isaac La Peyrère, for example. Spinoza, however, speaks directly without much clearing of his throat. The Swiss-Calvinist theologian Johann Heinrich Heidegger (1633 – 1698) recognized the erosion initiated by Hobbes and La Peyrère, "but no one," he writes, "struck at the foundations of the entire Pentateuch more shamelessly than Spinoza."[1] In essence, Spinoza's approach to biblical interpretation brought together the following assumptions: (1) The Bible is a product of human history and evolution and is to be read in the light of its natural history, and (2) philosophy and theology must be understood as two distinct dis-ciplines. The former discipline has to do with truth, and the latter with morality. For Spinoza, "the natural light of reason" became the primary lens for reading the Bible and negotiating its claims.

---

1. Quoted in Jonathan I. Israel, *Radical Enlightenment: Philosophy and the Making of Modernity 1650 – 1750* (New York: Oxford Univ. Press, 2001), 447. Steven Nadler writes, "Baruch (or Benedictus) de Spinoza (1632 – 77) was, without question, the most radical (and vilified) philosopher of his time" ("The Bible Hermeneutics of Baruch de Spinoza," in *Hebrew Bible/Old Testament: The History of Its Interpretation*, ed. Magne Saebø (Göttingen: Vandenhoeck & Ruprecht, 2008), 2:827.

When Spinoza first published his work advancing these ideas, he did so anonymously. The book's innocuous title was *Tractatus Theologico-Politicus* (1670).[2] The book's content was not so benign. The *Tractatus* met with immediate hostility and was formally banned in 1674.[3] Even before then, it was an illegal text whose publication was hindered.[4] In 1670, for example, the government ordered a raid on the bookshops of Leiden in a search-and-destroy mission against the *Tractatus*.[5] Before the publication of the *Tractatus*, his local Jewish community expelled him because of the kind of ideas presented in this volume. It is an understatement, therefore, to say that Spinoza's ideas and work created a stir.

It is important to come to terms with Spinoza because his work sets a trajectory for the modern-critical approach to Old Testament exegesis. With Spinoza, the search for the text's meaning becomes equated with the search for the text's ostensive historical referent, setting, and immediate intention. Moreover, his Old Testament interpretation is set within the framework of Cartesian modes of knowing, rejection of miracles, and denial of the supernatural.[6] As one can imagine, these modern intellectual instincts changed the rules of the interpretive game. Before turning our attention to Spinoza's work, we will explore a brief account of his life and intellectual/social context.

Crossing the Rubicon:
Spinoza's Cultural and Intellectual Setting

Spinoza was born on November 24, 1632, in Amsterdam, "the most beautiful city of Europe."[7] His parents, Michael de Espinoza and Hanna Debora, were Portuguese Jews who likely resettled in Amsterdam because of the

---

2. Published in English as *Theological-Political Treatise*, ed. J. Israel, trans. M. Silverthorne and J. Israel (Cambridge Texts in the History of Philosophy; Cambridge: Cambridge Univ. Press, 2007).

3. See Israel, *Radical Enlightenment*, 275.

4. "The notion that Spinoza's *Tractatus* ever circulated freely is thus a myth lacking all basis in fact" (Israel, *Radical Enlightenment*, 276). The illegal status of the *Tractatus* makes the wide dissemination of its first Latin and French editions all the more fascinating. The clandestine efforts for the book's publication are filled with intrigue and subversion. See Israel, *Radical Enlightenment*, chapter 16.

5. See Israel, *Radical Enlightenment*, 275–76.

6. The term *Cartesian* is shorthand for the rationalism associated with René Descartes. It is based on the Latin form of Descartes's name.

7. This description comes from the first biographical account of Spinoza, an account written anonymously (cited in Travis L. Frampton, *Spinoza and the Rise of Historical Criticism of the Bible* [London: T&T Clark, 2006], 122–23).

Portuguese Inquisition. The Jewish community in Amsterdam during this time was composed of three subgroups, each with its own synagogue and governing board.[8] In 1639 these three independent boards became one and were called the Talmud Torah.[9] Before this unification, however, both Benedict's father, Michael, and his uncle, Abraham, served on the governing board of their particular community (Beth Jacob). It is worth mentioning that only five people at a time served on these governing boards; it was an elite group. After the union of the three groups, Michael served on the Talmud Torah's board from 1649 – 1650.[10] The Espinoza family was respected and valued in Amsterdam's Jewish community. In time, Spinoza's rejection of the ideas and values of his community would bring shame on the Spinoza name.

There is debate among the sources regarding Spinoza's formal education and how he came into conflict with his Jewish community. He is often portrayed as a young scholar who debated with his rabbi on the finer points of biblical and Talmudic interpretation in the higher level *medrassim* (classes) of his rabbinic school. This is doubtful.[11] Spinoza's name does not appear on the class rolls kept during this time. This indicates a situation common to many young men of Spinoza's era. He probably joined his father's business while still an adolescent, precluding further education. In any case, it is unlikely Spinoza pursued formal, rabbinic education past the age of fourteen.[12] These events in no way cast aspersions on his gifted intellect. He had a masterful knowledge of the Hebrew language, along with specialized knowledge of the Scriptures and rabbinical sources.[13] Still, Spinoza's intellectual curiosity was left nearly unfettered once his formal, rabbinic training ceased.[14]

Spinoza continued as a merchant in his father's business for many years.

---

8. See Frampton, *Spinoza*, 125.

9. See Steven Nadler, *Spinoza: A Life* (Cambridge: Cambridge Univ. Press, 1999), 55.

10. See Frampton, *Spinoza*, 125.

11. See Frampton, *Spinoza*, 130 – 32. Rabbi Mortera's continued influence on his pupil, Spinoza, outside the Talmud Torah school has been helpfully pointed out by Nadler (*Spinoza*, 90 – 93). See also the possible influence of Rabbi Menasseh ben Israel, one of the most famous rabbis of the time, on Spinoza as well (Nadler, *Spinoza*, 93 – 100).

12. See Nadler, *Spinoza*, 63 – 64.

13. Ibid., 65. Nadler calls into question Spinoza's knowledge of the Talmud, describing it as "superficial at best" (*Spinoza*, 93).

14. This did not mean that all of Spinoza's education ceased. He most likely attended one of the community's schools for adults (*yeshiva*), but his formal, rabbinic training in the Talmud Torah school eventually came to an end (see Nadler, *Spinoza*, 89 – 91).

His business engagements with Protestant thinkers in the Netherlands may have exposed him to broader intellectual trends than the Talmud Torah community would have allowed. He also may have studied for a period at the University of Leiden (1656 – 1658), though the evidence for this is thin.[15] At any rate, Spinoza began to find the dogma of Judaism problematic and pursued other intellectual options.[16] He describes the immediate cause of his intellectual pursuit in his first published work, *Treatise on the Emendation of the Intellect.* He says his pursuits were born out of his experience that "all the things which regularly occur in ordinary life are empty and futile ..."[17] One can suppose Spinoza's business life left him intellectually bored while the traditional teachings of his rabbinic community became increasingly provincial and outdated. By his early twenties, his philosophical interests had turned decidedly secular.[18] His most influential tutor in this newfound intellectual freedom was René Descartes.[19]

Spinoza's continued repudiation of rabbinic teaching and authority led to an inevitable conflict. Israel describes the situation: "Ruined financially, Spinoza had now definitively made up his mind to cross the Rubicon — discarding respectability, social standing, and commerce and devoting himself wholeheartedly to philosophy."[20] The perfect storm came together in July 1656 as Spinoza's financial difficulties, which left him unable to pay a promissory tax, coincided with his adoption of new and offensive ideas.[21] A ban or *cherem* was placed against Spinoza and read out loud in the synagogue before the community.[22] Nadler writes, "There is no other excommunication document of the period marked by the vitriol directed at Spinoza when he was expelled from the congregation."[23] The cause of this hostility was most likely the controversial ideas Spinoza was embracing. As soon as four years after the ban, Spinoza's controversial ideas began to appear in published form. Some of the notions his religious commu-

---

15. See Israel, *Radical Enlightenment*, 172 – 73.

16. Nadler believes this dissatisfaction began as early as the age of fifteen (*Spinoza*, 100 – 101).

17. Nadler, *Spinoza*, 101.

18. See Nadler, *Spinoza*, 102.

19. See Nadler, *Spinoza*, 111 – 13; see also, Richard Popkin, *The History of Scepticism: From Savonarola to Bayle* (Oxford: Oxford Univ. Press, 2003), 239 – 53.

20. Israel, *Radical Enlightenment*, 171.

21. Frampton observes that historians have to speculate regarding the exact reasons that Spinoza was expelled from the community, though financial and intellectual/theological reasons are the ones most often suggested (*Spinoza*, 149 – 50); see also Nadler, *Spinoza*, 129 – 38.

22. The exact and stark wording of the ban can be found in Nadler, *Spinoza*, 120.

23. Nadler, *Spinoza*, 127.

nity found most offensive were the mortality of the soul, the denial of the Mosaic authorship of the Pentateuch, the rejection of the revelatory character of the Torah, and the dismissal of Israel's status as the elect of God.[24] Though religious apathy may have been tolerated in the Talmud Torah community, such heretical ideas as Spinoza's were a threat to the very fabric of their existence. After the ban, Baruch took the Christian name Benedictus. He no longer identified with his Jewish roots.

Our engagement with Spinoza is not meant to give a full biographical treatment.[25] To do so would take us too far afield. Our interest in Spinoza has to do primarily with his ideas and how they influenced biblical studies. But it is important to understand, even if somewhat minimally, the community values Spinoza was reacting against and the intellectual currents of the day that influenced his thought. Modernity's most cherished claims — autonomous intellectual pursuits, dismissal of dogmatic tradition, naturalism, and affirmation of the Cartesian "I" (I think therefore I am) — were advanced by Spinoza's philosophical and hermeneutical outlook. Because of these intellectual commitments, Spinoza inevitably clashed with his religious community, which valued divine revelation as the highest source of metaphysical and ethical knowledge.

Wood Stoves and the Autonomous I: Descartes's Early Influence on Spinoza

As mentioned above, Descartes was Spinoza's early teacher par excellence. As an aside, it is worth noting that Spinoza's philosophical system, "Spinozism," was the product of his own first-rate mind and should not be understood as "Descartes regurgitated." Jonathan Israel's discipline-defining work *Radical Enlightenment* identifies Spinoza as *the* major figure in the making of modernity. Nevertheless, Descartes's lasting influence on Spinoza is not questioned. Descartes's *Meditations on First Philosophy* (1641), *Principles of Philosophy* (1644), and the well-known *Discourse on Method* (1637) provided for Spinoza the philosophical grammar he needed to engage the dogmatism of his Jewish community and the larger Calvinist world he inhabited.[26] In many ways, Spinoza was more radical than Descartes because of his application of a Cartesian epistemology to the study

---

24. See Nadler, *Spinoza*, 131 – 32.
25. For such a treatment, see Nadler, *Spinoza*, and, especially, Israel, *Radical Enlightenment*.
26. See Nadler, *Spinoza*, 166.

of the Bible.[27] A brief overview of Descartes's theory of knowledge will help situate Spinoza's epistemological instincts.

From a "stove-heated room" in Germany, as the story goes, a twenty-three-year-old Descartes decided to rework the entirety of the Aristotelian philosophical tradition handed down to him in the schools—a system of thought already castigated by the medieval nominalists who preceded him.[28] Descartes's philosophical efforts were ambitious as he attempted to provide a secure foundation for knowledge. Where does authority reside in the sciences, and how is knowledge received? When everything else can be called into question, what is the unquestionable premise or foundation of reality and knowledge (e.g., *metaphysics*)? The unambiguous answer Descartes gives to this question is as follows: Whatever reality is or whatever I am, I can be certain that I am a thinking self. Our thinking, our ordering of knowledge—whether it corresponds to reality or not—is the foundation for metaphysical claims about reality and knowledge. This philosophical idea lead to Descartes's famous *Cogito: I think therefore I am* (*cogito ergo sum*).

In Descartes's *Meditations on First Philosophy* he raises the question, "What am I?" This question for Descartes is really about the broader and more important issue he is exploring, namely, "Of what can we be assured?" Before raising this question, Descartes reveals his willingness to tear down the edifice of knowledge handed down to him as he calls into question everything previously assumed.[29] Doubt creeps in at every level

---

27. See Popkin, *History of Scepticism*, 242.

28. See Robert Audi, ed., *The Cambridge Dictionary of Philosophy*, 2d ed. (Cambridge: Cambridge Univ. Press, 1999), 224; Michael Allen Gillespie, *The Theological Origins of Modernity* (Chicago: Univ. of Chicago Press, 2008), 188. Gillespie's account is especially illuminating and helpful. His work shows that Descartes was not the first to counter Aristotelianism or the belief that particular forms such as trees exist because of a prior universal form—a universal form that includes the variety present in the particulars, e.g., "treeness." Rather, Descartes is working within the skeptical fallout created by the medieval nominalist attacks on Aristotelian metaphysics and theology already established by the end of the fourteenth century. The nominalists challenged the Aristotelian notion of universals and sought to ground being in particulars and individuals. Descartes rejected the Aristotelian universal in favor of the governing and imposing categories of the mind. In other words, the mind, not universals, made sense of the multiplicity in the observable world (*Theological Origins*, ch. 1). See also Israel, *Radical Enlightenment*, 16 – 17.

29. "It is now some years since I detected how many were the false beliefs that I had from my earliest youth admitted as true, and how doubtful was everything I had since constructed on this basis; and from that time I was convinced that I must once for all seriously undertake to rid myself of all the opinions which I had formerly accepted, and commence to build anew from the foundation, if I wanted to establish any firm and permanent structure in the sciences" (quoted in E. S. Haldane and G. R. T. Ross, eds., *The Philosophical Works of Descartes* (Cambridge: Cambridge Univ. Press, 1973), 1144.

of metaphysical and physical inquiry.[30] Nothing he knows from tradition, culture, previous teachers, or religion can be taken for granted. Everything needs reconceptualization. So the question "What am I?" is predicated on Descartes's posture of doubt in relation to the world surrounding him and in relation to his own received knowledge.

"What am I?" could be answered in many different ways: I feel; I live; I breathe; I hear; I see. For Descartes, however, even the body itself and its sensory experiences can be doubted because it is a part of the material world surrounding us.[31] Our sensory experiences and feelings must also come under the umbrella of doubt.[32] Descartes illustrates the preceding with the experience of being near fire. Typically one describes being near fire with sensory descriptors. I see flames. I hear crackling. I feel heat. Though these experiences may be real and true experiences, Descartes is willing to grant to those skeptical of such sensory experiences — or of the claim that these experiences correspond to reality or assure us of their reality — that it is possible we are dreaming or that the experienced phenomenon is false. But what is not false, for Descartes, is the perception associated with our feelings. Even if the experience itself is not true, our thinking about it is. Listen to Descartes describe the situation in *Meditations*: "Let it be so [that we are dreaming]; still it is at least quite certain that it seems to me that I see light, that I hear noise, and that I feel heat. That cannot be false; properly speaking it is what is in me called feeling; and used in this precise sense that is no other thing than thinking."[33] So what is fundamentally true about being, and more specifically, about being human? What sort of thing is humanity? For Descartes, the unequivocal answer is we are "a thing which thinks."[34] Our minds govern every other aspect of our being human, in particular, our passions and our

---

30. Again, religious skepticism was fully operative at this time because of the nominalist controversies. As this pertains to Descartes, see Gillespie, *Theological Origins*, 170–206.

31. See Charles Taylor, *Sources of the Self: The Making of the Modern Identity* (Cambridge, Mass.: Harvard Univ. Press, 1989), 145.

32. On Descartes's relationship to the history of scepticism, see Popkin, *History of Scepticism*, 143–73.

33. Quoted in Haldane and Ross, *Works of Descartes*, 1:153.

34. "I am, I exist, that is certain. But how often? Just when I think; for it might possibly be the case if I ceased entirely to think, that I should likewise cease altogether to exist. I do not now admit anything which is not necessarily true: to speak accurately I am not more than a thing which thinks, that is to say a mind or a soul, or an understanding, or a reason, which are terms whose significance was formerly unknown to me. I am, however, a real thing and really exist; but what thing? I have answered: a thing which thinks" (quoted in Haldane and Ross, *Works of Descartes*, 1:151–52).

experiences.[35] Authority is now located in the human subject. This turn toward the human subject is the central tenet of modernity.

As complicated as the previous section is — Descartes is more so! — what one notes about Descartes and his placement within the history of ideas is the movement of rationality (moreover, a rationality objectively detached from the phenomenal world around us) to the center of the physical and metaphysical world. Our thinking, our ordering of perceived experiences and external phenomena, shapes reality. It provides the assured and confident foundation for our inquiry into matters outside of ourselves. The one thing we can be assured of is our own ability to think, that is, to categorize in clear and distinct ways.[36] This does not mean Descartes leaves no room for empirical testing in his scientific approach to the material world. What it does mean is that the assured foundation of our knowledge when engaging the sciences is located in our innate ideas. Great amounts of confidence are heaped onto what Descartes (and Spinoza) calls "natural light" or the "light of reason."[37] Here, indeed, we have a fundamental shift in the history of ideas away from the substance of things themselves or the conclusions drawn from rational inquiry (e.g., Plato and Aristotle's universals) to the actual thinking process itself.[38] Method begins to reign supreme.

Descartes did believe that rationality and faith could happily coincide with one another.[39] Therefore, it would be unfair to describe Descartes as an atheist or as antireligious. What Descartes did do in the search for methodological certainty, however, was cut the cord of reason from faith or revelation.[40] Descartes may not have been a Deist, but his emphasis on self-sufficiency, natural reason, and the confidence in autonomous rationality

---

35. See Taylor, *Sources of the Self,* 150–51.

36. This distinction between the external world and the thinking self, known as Cartesian dualism, is key to understanding Descartes's philosophical approach. Descartes divides the world between extended substances (*res extensa*) — this is the material world around us — and thinking substances (*res cogitans*). These two are independent of each other (see Audi, ed., *Cambridge Dictionary of Philosophy,* 226).

37. See ibid., 226.

38. Taylor states, "For Descartes [as opposed to Plato], rationality means thinking according to certain canons. The judgment now turns on properties of the activity of thinking rather than on the substantive beliefs which emerge from it" (*Sources of the Self,* 157).

39. Eventually, Descartes's marriage between faith and rationality would become untenable, e.g., Kant's critique of reason and the displacement of knowledge in the experienced/phenomenal world from the noumenal world that goes beyond the physical arena of experience.

40. For an in-depth analysis of Descartes's turn to the subject in light of the intellectual context of his day, see Gillespie, *Theological Origins,* 170–206.

severed faith from reason and led to Deistic results. God, theology, and religion were left to one sphere, while the rational and autonomous self in quest of a reliable and transferable method was hermetically sealed in its own philosophical world. We will see the effects of this bifurcation in Spinoza's hermeneutic. Charles Taylor clarifies, "The truth behind the anachronistic judgments [that Descartes is a Deist] ... is that this new conception of inwardness, an inwardness of self-sufficiency, of autonomous powers of ordering by reason, *also* prepared the ground for modern unbelief."[41] Spinoza's emphasis on the "natural light of reason" in the quest for truth set a course for the academic study of the Bible. His tendencies are observed to this day.[42]

Spinoza and the Search for the Bible's Meaning: The *Tractatus*

Spinoza's *Tractatus* is a targeted attempt at defusing religious obscurantism, placing philosophical rationality at the pinnacle of human knowing and setting forth a political ideal that created the necessary intellectual space for various viewpoints to be affirmed in a free society. Much of Spinoza's political theory plants the seeds for democratic societies now taken for granted in most of the Western world.

During much of the first half of the seventeenth century, the religious and political zealotry of the Thirty Years War had ravaged Europe. The historical context for much of Spinoza's political and ethical concerns is located in this sociopolitical nightmare in European history. Spinoza believes societies should be governed by a rational/free-thinking kind of morality rather than religiously governed political/ethical systems. Religious dogmatism, military might, and political ambition made for a toxic combination throughout the Thirty Years War.[43] The treaty of Westphalia, which brought an end to the Thirty Years Wars, was signed in 1648 — eight years before Spinoza's ban. Therefore, the influence of wars launched

---

41. Taylor, *Sources of the Self*, 157–58.

42. Spinoza was not a slavish follower of Descartes's philosophical system and could be critical of its particularities. Spinoza's philosophy was its own worked-out system, though it shared much in common with Cartesian epistemology. In fact, as Israel has demonstrated, Spinoza's philosophical mind and work was far more influential in shaping modernity than Descartes's (see Israel, *Radical Enlightenment*, 162–66).

43. For an overview of the political and religious complex associated with the Thirty Years War, see Joseph Bergin, ed., *The Seventeenth Century: Europe 1598–1715* (Short Oxford History of Europe; Oxford: Oxford Univ. Press, 2008), 112–44.

in the name of religious zealotry is significant for Spinoza's political and philosophical thought. This sociohistorical context also creates some sympathy for Spinoza's project. The Western world had been turned upside down in the name of religion attached to the machinations of national politics.

Spinoza's historical context sheds light on his political motivation to see society freed from the tyranny of religious obscurantism. Authority was dislocated from religious spheres and suspicion was directed at political systems that mingled religion and politics. This dislocation created intellectual holes in the political, philosophical, and theological arenas. Spinoza's larger philosophical project is a concentrated attempt at filling them. Our level of engagement with Spinoza is more modest and limited as we seek to understand the contours of his approach to Scripture and its interpretation. Therefore, I will give attention primarily to hermeneutical matters. It is, however, important to remember that Spinoza's hermeneutical instincts are located within a much broader philosophical and political world.

We will explore three issues in an attempt to understand the philosophical and hermeneutical moves Spinoza makes when attending to Scripture. First, we will examine Spinoza's understanding of the autonomy of human rationality and the necessary distinction of philosophy and theology/biblical studies. Put simply, theology has to do with morality, and philosophy has to do with truth. To conflate these two is to confuse the particular form of knowledge each sphere yields. Next, we will engage Spinoza's understanding of the nature of Scripture. The prophets of the Old Testament will provide a window into his understanding of Scripture's nature. Spinoza raises questions such as: Are the Scriptures authoritative? If so, on what matters do they function authoritatively? Finally, we will explore Spinoza's understanding of biblical interpretation and the interpreter's quest for the author's intention in his immediate situation. Throughout most of the *Tractatus*, Spinoza is really asking the following questions: What exactly is the Bible, and how is it to be understood by means of the natural light of reason?

Mind, Method, and the Necessary Distinction of Philosophy and Theology

Spinoza prizes rationality and is unfettered in his praise of humanity's ability to reason independently of extraneous norms, religious or otherwise. Rejecting the subordination of philosophy to theology, Spinoza declares forthrightly, "I am amazed that it should not be thought a crime to speak disparagingly of the mind, *the true text of God's word*, and then to proclaim it corrupt, blind, and depraved, while deeming it the highest offense to think such things of the mere letter and image of God's word."[44] Spinoza understands the text of one's mind as the place where truth has been written by God. Spinoza here is making a case for the mind's inspiration in the face of other competing norms. Human rationality located in the autonomous mind is the source for truth. Scripture, on the other hand, plays a different and more minimal role for Spinoza.

Spinoza continues, "They consider it pious not to trust their reason and their own judgment and deem it impious to have doubts concerning the reliability of those who have handed down the sacred books to us. This is plain stupidity, not piety."[45] In a sense, Spinoza has taken off his gloves at this point in the argument. For Spinoza, it is pure folly to allow the Bible an authoritative voice in philosophical investigation. The glaring weaknesses of the Bible are too many to overcome. When compared and contrasted with the achievements of modern humanity, the Bible appears even more fragile and insipid.

Spinoza's confidences are in human rationality, while his skepticism works overtime when the Bible makes claims about being, God's nature, knowledge, or the mechanics of the universe. These matters are philosophical, not theological. In fairness to Spinoza, he considers the authority of the Bible in its more limited role an important matter. His understanding of Scripture's nature and claims, however, is in the end subordinated to human, intellectual autonomy. Where there is conflict between human rationality and biblical claims, the former outweighs the latter. The presumptive authority of the past is replaced with a confidence in human progress, thought, and method.

Imbibing a Cartesian denial of the past's authority and claims, Spinoza seeks out a secure foundation both in the realm of philosophical reason and religion. The table of knowledge regarding the Scriptures' authority and nature had to be cleared in an attempt to understand Scripture properly for the first time. With language sounding remarkably similar to Descartes's opening paragraph of *Meditations on First Philosophy*, Spinoza

---

44. Spinoza, *Theological-Political Treatise*, 188.
45. Ibid., 182.

states, "I resolved in all seriousness to make a fresh examination of Scripture *with a free and unprejudiced mind,* and to assert nothing about it, and to accept nothing as its teaching, which I did not quite clearly derive from it" (emphasis mine).[46] I will borrow language from the Reformation to illustrate Spinoza's move here. He turns *sola scriptura* into *nuda scriptura,* that is, Scripture stripped of any theological or ecclesial context. In effect, *sola scriptura* is reduced to the individual's own interpretive instincts and guidelines. Now the Scriptures and their authority must be understood on their own, with no recourse to the churchly or theological context in which Scripture is received. Hilary of Poitiers's claim that "those who are situated outside the church are not able to acquire any understanding of the divine discourse" is in principle dismissed by Spinoza because of the infringement such a claim has on the independence and autonomy of a free-thinking and rational reader.[47]

What exactly are the theological strictures from which Spinoza is seeking to free himself? He clarifies:

> This is also clear from the fact that most of them [those who simply assent to the truthfulness of Scripture] take it as a fundamental principle ... that Scripture is true and divine throughout. But of course this is the very thing that should emerge from a critical examination and understanding of Scripture. It would be much better to derive it from Scripture itself, which has no need of human fabrications, but they assume it at the very beginning as a rule of interpretation.[48]

Spinoza's work marks a significant shift as the premodern now elides into the modern period of biblical interpretation. A pre-understanding, or confession, about the nature of Scripture on the front side of the interpretive process creates an interpretive brick wall for Spinoza.

It should be noted that modernity's biblical scholars were not the first to see "problems" within the Bible needing to be resolved. One may read Calvin on the authorship of 2 Peter or Augustine's engagement of Genesis 6 in *The City of God* to recognize this is the case.[49] The interpretive shift between the premodern and modern period has more to do with the prop-

---

46. Ibid., 8 – 9, emphasis mine.

47. Quoted in David S. Yeago, "The Bible," in *Knowing the Triune God: The Work of the Spirit in the Practice of the Church,* ed. J. F. Buckley and D. S. Yeago (Grand Rapids: Eerdmans, 2001), 49.

48. Ibid.

49. In this sense, John Barton is right to deny that critical engagement of the Scriptures is a novum of modernity (*The Nature of Biblical Criticism* [Louisville: Westminster John Knox, 2007], 11).

erly basic role faith and belief play in one's theological epistemology. For Augustine and Calvin, the revelatory and inspired character of Scripture is assumed when they engage the problems of the Bible. With Anselm, the precritical exegetical tradition understands belief to precede knowledge (*credo ut intelligam*). For Spinoza, and John Locke who follows, belief in the truthfulness of the Bible is necessarily suspended until matters can be resolved rationally by a method that can provide warrant or justification for the Bible's trustworthiness.[50] No longer is one's confession regarding the Bible's divine source properly basic, with our own reason and methods having to be brought into accord with this confession.[51] Now the autonomous mind, its own preoccupation with transferable methods from the sciences into the humanities, and the desire for general and universal laws are moved to the center. Scripture must accord itself with this norm.

This is the intellectual context of Spinoza's desire for a "prejudice-free" approach to the study of the Scriptures. Only such an approach can preserve the integrity of the Bible from external norms. This is important to remember as we engage Spinoza's thought. He *is* concerned about the authority of Scripture. Spinoza is not dismissing the Bible's role in religion and even public discourse. But as one turns to nature itself with a free and unfettered mind for the sake of knowing the substance of nature as it really is, so too must one turn to the Scriptures with a cleared mind for the sake of understanding what Scripture is.

The only prejudice or presupposition not called into question for Spinoza — his properly basic belief that is not argued for but is in fact assumed — is the mind's priority and ability to analyze and codify Scripture according to its own nature. As Irenaeus in the early church argued for the necessity of a *regula fidei* (rule of faith) to understand the mind of Scripture as a whole, so too Spinoza argues for a *regula* or a guide.[52] For Spinoza, this guide is what he calls *the natural light of reason*. It is not divine revelation or the triune character of God or the soteriological/

---

50. For a helpful articulation of this epistemological move in modernity, see Neil B. MacDonald, "Illocutionary Stance in Hans Frei's *The Eclipse of Biblical Narrative*: An Exercise in Conceptual Redescription and Normative Analysis," in *After Pentecost: Language and Biblical Interpretation*; ed. Craig Bartholomew, Colin Greene, and Karl Möller (Scripture and Hermeneutics Series; Grand Rapids: Zondervan, 2001), 2:312–28.

51. See Alvin Plantinga, *Warranted Christian Belief* (New York: Oxford Univ. Press, 2000), chapter 12.

52. On the *regula fidei*, see John Behr, *The Way to Nicaea* (Formation of Christian Theology; Crestwood, N.Y.: St. Vladimir's Seminary Press, 2001), 17–48.

christological context of Scripture that functions as a guide for those who read it. These categories obscure rather than enlighten. Rather, the final arbiter in the process of interpretation and application is the natural light of reason.

In fairness to Spinoza, he would not have articulated the matter in this way. Spinoza actually claims a neutral stance when reading the Scriptures. For example, at the end of the preface to the *Tractatus*, Spinoza claims that we must derive all of our knowledge of Scripture and the spiritual matters it contains from the Scriptures themselves with no intrusion from "what we discover by the natural light of reason."[53] Such an account serves Spinoza's effort to make philosophy and religion distinct categories. In fact, John Sandys-Wunsch's reading of the *Tractatus* underscores Spinoza's primary interest as the separation of philosophy and religion.[54] The first six chapters of the *Tractatus* guard philosophy from the intrusion of religion, and chapters 7–11 protect religion or the study of the Bible from the intrusion of philosophy. In chapters 12–15 he presents a positive account of the nature and claims of Scripture.[55] Therefore, within Spinoza's articulation, the natural light of reason and the claims of religion are distinct categories. With this said, however, even a superficial reading of Spinoza's work reveals that such neat and clear categories are not functional, or possible, for Spinoza. Wittingly or unwittingly, the natural light of reason governs Spinoza's attempts to derive from Scripture itself an understanding of its true nature.

Spinoza is indeed concerned to protect philosophy, with its recourse to the natural light of reason, and religion, with its more limited claims regarding morality and piety, from confusion or conflation. At the same time, what is surely the case for Spinoza is that the mind of the autonomous reader with its properly crafted and assured methods is the governing norm for conclusions in both philosophy and religion.

In chapter 15, a pivotal chapter of the *Tractatus*, Spinoza states:

> Those who do not know how to distinguish philosophy from theology dispute as to whether Scripture should be subject to reason or whether, on the contrary, reason should be the servant of Scripture: that is to say, whether the sense of Scripture should be accommodated

---

53. Spinoza, *Theological-Political Treatise*, 10.
54. John Sandys-Wunsch, "Spinoza—The First Biblical Theologian," *ZAW* 93 (1981): 334.
55. Ibid.

to reason or whether reason should be subordinated to Scripture. The latter position is adopted by skeptics who deny the certainty of reason, and the former defended by dogmatists. But from what we have previously said it is obvious that both are absolutely wrong. For whichever position we adopt, we would have to distort either reason or Scripture since we have demonstrated that the Bible does not teach philosophical matters but only piety, and everything in Scripture is adapted to the understanding and preconceptions of the common people.[56]

Inherent within such a claim is Spinoza's self-assured starting point: reason must recognize that the Bible does not make philosophical or metaphysical claims. Even in an attempt to come to grips with what the Bible *says about itself*, certain philosophical presuppositions are assumed and function as hermeneutical guides in the search for the Bible's own self-understanding. For example, one such assumption is a deistic or general understanding of providence with its "fixed and unalterable order of nature and the interconnectedness of [all] things."[57]

Deeply ingrained in Spinoza's framework of Bible reading is a notion of divine accommodation in which God adapts his message to simpler minds of a bygone era.[58] It is the task of the modern interpreter to separate the wheat from the chaff when reading the Scriptures. The presumptive authority of the past is replaced with the self-confident modern interpreter along with their assumed, indubitable, and universal laws of reason: seas do not split and prophets do not hear directly from God.[59] In this pivotal chapter of the *Tractatus*, Spinoza closes his case for the necessary separation of philosophy from religion. He concludes, "It is indeed true that Scripture must be explained by Scripture, so long as we are only deriving the sense of the passages and the meaning of the prophets, but after we have arrived at the true sense, we must necessarily use our judgment and reason before giving assent to it."[60] If a claim made by the Scriptures comes into conflict with reason, Spinoza is forced to reject it. By making this interpretive move, he believes the integrity of both philosophy and religion

---

56. Spinoza, *Theological-Political Treatise*, 186.

57. Ibid., 44. See Sandys-Wunsch ("The First Biblical Theologian," 333) regarding the different ways Spinoza uses reason within the *Tractatus*.

58. Spinoza, *Theological-Political Treatise*, 40.

59. We will see the outworking of these sensibilities in the section on Spinoza's understanding of the prophets.

60. Spinoza, *Theological-Political Treatise*, 187 – 88.

are preserved. Once this winnowing interpretive process is complete, one is left with a Bible stripped to its moral and charitable components. This moral reduction is especially evident in Spinoza's handling of the Old Testament prophets.

Prophetic Imagination and Scripture's Religion: Morality and Justice

Spinoza is frank about his antipathy for superstition. The first line of the *Tractatus* is indicative of this antipathy: "If men were always able to regulate their affairs with sure judgment, they would not get caught up in any superstition."[61] For Spinoza, the prophets of the Old Testament have too long been understood superstitiously. Even revelation itself can be conceived of as superstitious because we know, or at least Spinoza knows, that only Moses spoke with God face-to-face. Only Moses heard a "real voice" from God.[62] Every other prophet besides the archetypal prophet Moses received their prophecy via words or images.[63] With the prophets, interference is run between divine communication and prophetic reception because they receive prophetic knowledge from words and images rather than their minds or rationality. What then makes a prophet a prophet? It is the gift of imagination.

When the Scriptures speak about the Spirit of God being poured out on a prophet, these claims are an accommodation to the simple minds of common people. They are not claims about the character of revelation coming to a prophet by God's own Spirit. Direct communication can only take place body to body, as with Moses alone, or mind to mind, as with Jesus alone. The language of being filled with the Spirit is an internal claim about the prophet's uniquely cultivated piety and virtue. Revelation in such an account becomes religious self-awareness. Spinoza does claim that within the prophet's imaginative gifts genuine divine communication can take place. Therefore, Spinoza does not dismiss the veracity of prophetic knowledge. As natural knowledge has its source in the mind, prophetic knowledge has its source in the imagination.[64] But both sorts of knowledge are an act of self-discovery.

---

61. Ibid., 3.
62. Ibid., 15.
63. Ibid., 19. The pinnacle of divine communication is found in Christ, who communicated with God *mind to mind*.
64. Ibid., 24–25.

What kind of knowledge is derived then from prophetic knowledge? Spinoza spends the entirety of chapter 2 answering this question. Because those who are gifted with reason tend to suppress their imaginative side (or are not very good at it) and because those who are gifted with imagination tend to have less facility with their rational faculties, Spinoza concludes that "those who look in the book of the prophets for wisdom and a knowledge of natural and spiritual things are completely on the wrong track."[65] Why? Because prophetic knowledge depends on the imagination alone. Therefore, it is vulnerable to all the problems one might associate with the imagination, namely, its capricious and subjective nature because of differing personality types, disposition, gifts, temperament, and assumed beliefs.[66] The type of certainty one might expect from the prophets is not mathematical certainty, which is only available to the natural light of reason. To illustrate this uncertainty, Spinoza points to the prophets' need for a sign to authenticate the word of the Lord — a point Spinoza illustrates briefly but assumes universally.[67] Natural knowledge, on the other hand, provides certainty by its very nature.[68] What we receive from the prophets then is a tendentious type of knowledge that is not as certain as knowledge gained rationally.

As mentioned above, Spinoza is crafting an argument for the separation of philosophy and religion. The prophets provide a case in point of his overarching agenda. He states, "I think this question is of major importance, for I ultimately conclude from it that prophecy never made the prophets more learned, but left them with their preconceived beliefs and that, for this reason, we are in no way obliged to believe them in purely philosophical matters."[69] Truth is a "purely philosophical" category, and the prophets of the Old Testament are not a source for truth. The prophets of the Old Testament are looked to for the proper "method and manner of obedience that is the dogma of true piety and faith."[70] The result is the following schema: philosophy is concerned with truth; religion is concerned with morality.

---

65. Ibid., 27.

66. Ibid., 30.

67. "Scripture does not always actually mention a sign, but we must nevertheless suppose that the prophets always had one" (*Theological-Political Treatise*, 29).

68. Spinoza, *Theological-Political Treatise*, 28.

69. Ibid., 33.

70. Ibid., 190.

Spinoza's engagement of the prophets is much fuller and more robust than the account given here. Moreover, I acknowledge the complex matters one must address when it comes to the philosophical claims of the Old Testament. Even those who affirm the trustworthiness of the Bible allow for flexibility when the Old Testament figures speak of natural events (like the sun rising) from the standpoint of their own observation. In other words, a certain literary and theological sensitivity should allow the Bible to do what the Bible claims to be doing. In one sense, this is exactly what Spinoza seeks — an understanding of the ontology of the Bible from the vantage point of reason's indubitable center.

In another and more important sense, Spinoza's naturalist understanding of the world does demand the removal of revelation as a normative category in biblical theology.[71] Though Spinoza claims to be reading the Scriptures with a free and unprejudiced mind, in fact Spinoza does know in advance what the Bible cannot do and be. *It cannot contradict what is known from the natural light of reason.* In this sense, the natural light of reason functions as the normative guide for the reading of Scripture.

The modern desire for universal or general laws based on unshaken foundations does run into conflict with a book like the Old Testament. It is, after all, a book that affirms God's revealing of himself in his election and covenant dealings with a particular people called Israel.[72] Without denying the difficult hermeneutical work involved in the following process, it is a fundamental claim within Christian theology that first order God-talk does flow from one's engagement with the Bible's narrative, prophetic, and poetic literature.[73] Spinoza's desire for the general and universal blushes in the face of the Old Testament's particularity. What, then, is one left with in the search for the general in the face of the particular? One is left with a Bible reduced to its moral function alone.

If Spinoza's approach to the Bible demands a proper method that

---

71. Spinoza's panentheistic understanding of the relationship between God and nature is beyond the scope of this chapter. For more on this, see Jonathan Israel's *Radical Enlightenment.*

72. "Belief in a historical narrative, however reliable it may be, can give us no knowledge of God or consequently love of God either. For love of God arises from knowledge of him; and knowledge of him has to be drawn from universal notions which are certain in themselves and well-known, and so it is by no means the case that belief in a historical narrative is a necessary requirement for us to reach our highest good" (*Theological-Political Treatise,* 61).

73. For a robust theological account of Scripture's role in the divine economy, see John Webster, "Resurrection and Scripture," in *Christology and Scripture: Interdisciplinary Perspectives,* ed. A. T. Lincoln and A. Paddison (London: T&T Clark, 2008), 138–55.

guarantees knowledge of the Bible's own nature, then what exactly is his hermeneutic?

Hermeneutics, Meaning, and the Search for the Original Situation

In an effort to preserve the integrity of the Bible from philosophical encroachment, Spinoza provides a hermeneutic meant to safeguard the Bible's meaning. He expends a great deal of effort in the *Tractatus* to prove that the Bible is a natural document with a natural history. Our engagement with Spinoza in the previous section focused on his natural understanding of prophecy. Spinoza's efforts are broader in scope than prophecy alone. He aims to reveal the natural history of the Pentateuch (denying the general Mosaic authorship of the Pentateuch); he places divine law in naturalist categories and denies miracles because of a fixed and unalterable understanding of nature. Even Israel's election by God was not an indication of Israel's unique status vis-à-vis the nations. Rather, Israel's election is the necessary language for establishing and maintaining her statehood and material welfare. In effect, Israel was no different from the surrounding nations.

Nadler observes that Spinoza's innovative reading of the Old Testament is not in his calling into question the Mosaic authorship of the Pentateuch or his understanding of Scripture's compositional genesis as "transmitted through a fallible historical process."[74] Others before Spinoza had made similar claims. Rather, "Spinoza's radical and innovative claim was to argue that this holds great significance for how Scripture is to be read and interpreted."[75] Spinoza's efforts are an impressive and all-encompassing account of the humanity of Scripture under the norms of a natural, human process of innovation and fallibility.

If, then, the Scriptures are natural documents detached from superstition, then one must interpret them as a natural document. Spinoza states:

> To formulate the matter succinctly, I hold that the method of interpreting Scripture does not differ from the [correct] method of interpreting nature, but rather is wholly consonant with it. The [correct] method of interpreting nature consists above all in constructing a natural history,

---

74. Nadler, "Biblical Hermeneutics of Baruch de Spinoza," 831.
75. Ibid.

from which we derive the definitions of natural things, as from certain data. Likewise, to interpret Scripture, we need to assemble a genuine history of it and to deduce the thinking of the Bible's authors by valid inferences from this history, as from certain data and principles.[76]

As knowledge of nature is derived from nature alone, so too must our understanding of the Bible be grasped from its nature alone. Nature's principles are derived from universal laws found within our innate ideas. The Scripture's natural history is to be understood from the historical excavation of the author's original intention in the text's historic setting. With the discovery of the author's intention comes the discovery of the text's meaning. One must recall, however, that meaning does not necessarily have to do with truth. Truth is a philosophical category.

How, then, does one recover this original authorial intention? First, knowledge of Hebrew is a necessity. Second, one must categorize the various claims made by the biblical books themselves while seeking to observe contradictions and difficulties. Spinoza warns the interpreter not to allow his own reason to temper the claims Scripture is making. Reason will come in later when the interpreter accepts or rejects the various claims. Third, historical inquiry must take into account the social and personal circumstances of the biblical author, the occasion for writing, the audience, the language of writing, and the "fate of each book." For proper historical understanding of biblical books, according to Spinoza, one must have a securely reconstructed historical background of the text's author and audience. Also, one must know the textual history and reception of the text both in its compositional and canonical reception. A desire for a proper and stable method of interpretation is Spinoza's primary interest. Only such a method can overcome the problems of divergent, traditional readings.[77] Spinoza's method is a quest for catholic objectivity.

Spinoza knows his interpretive method is a tall order. After outlining the method, he then rehearses the interpretive problems inherent in each step. For example, knowledge of the historical meaning of texts demands knowledge of Hebrew. Well, Spinoza recognizes that our knowledge of classical Hebrew is spotty in places. In effect, Spinoza gives with one hand and takes away with the other. In an effort to provide a secure foundation for interpretation based on the author's intentions, Spinoza pulls the

---

76. Spinoza, *Theological-Political Treatise*, 98.
77. See Plantinga, *Warranted Christian Belief*, 386 – 87, 398 – 99.

rug out from biblical interpretation because of the difficulties of securing confident knowledge in all three steps of the process. He observes, "I think these difficulties are so great that I do not hesitate to affirm that in numerous passages either we do not know the true sense of Scripture or can only guess at it without any assurance."[78] Spinoza's historicist approach is the only method that will engender confidence in interpretive conclusions. At the same time, he recognizes the enormous challenges at play in every level of the hermeneutical process. Spinoza concludes, "Moreover, I do not doubt that everyone now sees that this method requires no other light than that of natural reason."[79]

Conclusion

Within the history of Old Testament criticism, a significant shift took place with Spinoza. A naturalist understanding of Scripture, with no recourse to its theological or ecclesiastical setting, demands a naturalist reading of the text. What is a naturalist reading? It is a reading where the literal sense of Scripture is collapsed into the historical sense. The text becomes sealed in the world where it was born. As such, the Bible is to be read as any other book born out of a particular time and place. It is deemed superstitious to understand Scripture as the living voice of God. Even more problematic is allowing such a confession a constraining role in the interpretive process. The indubitable foundation for the proper understanding of Scripture is the historical reconstruction of the author and his original recipients. The literal sense *is* the historical sense.[80]

As we move forward in our picture gallery study, we will observe how central this historicist shift was in the modern reading of the Old Testament. This is not to reduce modern critical study of the Old Testament to historical matters alone: attention to literary matters such as genre and poetics are advanced in the modern period as well. But the impulse to understand the success of interpretation by historical or literary reconstruction of the text becomes a trademark of modern criticism. With

---

78. Spinoza, *Theological-Political Treatise*, 110.

79. Ibid., 111.

80. A helpful account of the move within modernity to conflate the literal sense of Scripture with the historical sense is Brevard Childs, "The *Sensus Literalis* of Scripture: An Ancient and Modern Problem," in *Beiträge zur Altestamentalichen Theologie: Festschrift für Walther Zimmerli zum 70 Geburtstag*, ed. H. Donner, R. Hanhart, and R. Smend (Göttingen: Vandenhoeck & Ruprecht, 1977), 80–93.

Spinoza, the Hebrew Scriptures are henceforth understood as a source for the critical retrieval of Israel's past and/or religious outlook.

FOR FURTHER READING

Barton, John. *The Nature of Biblical Criticism*. Louisville: Westminster John Knox, 2007.

Frampton, Travis L. *Spinoza and the Rise of Historical Criticism of the Bible*. London: T&T Clark, 2006.

Gillespie, Michael Allen. *The Theological Origins of Modernity*. Chicago: Univ. of Chicago Press, 2008.

Israel, Jonathan I. *Radical Enlightenment: Philosophy and the Making of Modernity* 1650 – 1750. New York: Oxford Univ. Press, 2001.

MacDonald, Neil B. "Illocutionary Stance in Hans Frei's *The Eclipse of Biblical Narrative*: An Exercise in Conceptual Redescription and Normative Analysis." Pages 312 – 28 in *After Pentecost: Language and Biblical Interpretation*. Volume 2 of Scripture and Hermeneutics Series. Edited by Craig Bartholomew, Colin Greene, and Karl Möller. Grand Rapids: Zondervan, 2001.

Nadler, Steven. "The Biblical Hermeneutics of Baruch de Spinoza." Pages 827 – 36 in *Hebrew Bible/Old Testament: The History of Its Interpretation*, II. Edited by Magne Saebø. Göttingen: Vandenhoeck & Ruprecht, 2008.

———. *Spinoza: A Life*. Cambridge: Cambridge Univ. Press, 1999.

Plantinga, Alvin. *Warranted Christian Belief*. New York: Oxford Univ. Press, 2000.

Sandys-Wunsch, John. "Spinoza — The First Biblical Theologian." *Zeitschrift für die Alttestamentliche Wissenschaft* 93 (1981): 327 – 41.

Taylor, Charles. *Sources of the Self: The Making of the Modern Identity*. Cambridge, Mass.: Harvard Univ. Press, 1989.

Webster, John. "Resurrection and Scripture." Pages 138 – 55 in *Christology and Scripture: Interdisciplinary Perspectives*. Edited by A. T. Lincoln and A. Paddison. London: T&T Clark, 2008.

Yeago, David S. "The Bible." Pages 49 – 93 in *Knowing the Triune God: The Work of the Spirit in the Practice of the Church*. Edited by J. F. Buckley and D. S. Yeago. Grand Rapids: Eerdmans, 2001.

W. M. L. DE WETTE

(1780–1849)

History Becomes Religion

BENEDICT SPINOZA PAVED THE WAY FOR A HISTORICIST AND NATURALIST approach to reading Scripture. A tectonic shift in biblical studies was taking place as confessional approaches to reading Scripture were replaced in the academy with decidedly nonconfessional ones. After scholars placed divine revelation on the margins, they then sought for the proper intellectual location for biblical studies. This location tended to be literary and historical; the former related to an appreciation of the philological and poetic elements of the Old Testament and the latter to the text's prehistory and immediate historical setting.[1]

Most Old Testament professors in Germany in the mid to late eighteenth century espoused a rationalist hermeneutic.[2] Following the trajectory set by Spinoza, figures such as Johann Salomo Semler (1725–1791) and Johann David Michaelis (1717–1791) approached the exegesis of the Old Testament on the basis of grammatical and philological analysis, an appreciation of the ancient world out of which the Old Testament arose, and a denial of the Christian dogmatic understanding of biblical inspiration.[3] "The academic lecture and the sermon are so different," stated

---

1. For a detailed and illuminating account of early modernity's academic engagement with the Bible, see Jonathan Sheehan, *The Enlightenment Bible: Translation, Scholarship, Culture* (Princeton: Princeton Univ. Press, 2005).

2. See John Rogerson, *Old Testament Criticism in the Nineteenth Century: England and Germany* (Minneapolis: Fortress, 1985), 16.

3. See Rogerson, *Old Testament Criticism,* 16–17; J. C. O'Neill, *The Bible's Authority: A Portrait Gallery of Thinkers from Lessing to Bultmann* (Edinburgh: T&T Clark, 1991), 39–53.

Michaelis, "that, if done well, they will in time only corrupt one another."[4] Michaelis believed that thorough philological analysis of the Old Testament would raise ancient Israel to the classical status of Greece and Rome. If the Old Testament were to retain a venerated status in German culture, it would only do so as a classic text, not a scriptural text.[5] Semler and Michaelis are only two representatives of much larger trends taking place in various quarters of European universities in the eighteenth century.[6] In effect, the academic study of the Bible was moving from the theology faculty to the history and classics departments.[7]

Few biblical scholars of the late eighteenth and early nineteenth century advanced this modern approach more than Wilhelm Martin Leberecht de Wette. As will be seen, describing de Wette as "historicist" in method does not reflect the philosophical complexity of his "historicist" approach or his understanding of the kind of history to be found in the Bible. Despite de Wette's obscurity within academic discourse today — Schleiermacher, a contemporary and colleague of de Wette's, is the better known of the two — de Wette's influence on nineteenth-century biblical studies can hardly be overestimated. Karl Barth wondered if under differing historical circumstances de Wette would have actually eclipsed Schleiermacher as the great theologian of the nineteenth century.[8] During de Wette's own time, he was an intellectual luminary who stood shoulder to shoulder with the better known figures of the day — Hegel, Fichte, and, as mentioned, Schleiermacher. In fact, Julius Wellhausen said of him, "A clever fellow! You can already find everything I have done in the Old Testament in him."[9]

---

4. Quoted in Michael C. Legaspi, *The Death of Scripture and the Rise of Biblical Studies* (Oxford Studies in Historical Theology; New York: Oxford Univ. Press, 2010), 27.

5. Again, see Legaspi's thorough review of Michaelis's views (*The Death of Scripture and the Rise of Biblical Studies*).

6. See especially Hans W. Frei, *The Eclipse of Biblical Narrative: A Study in Eighteenth and Nineteenth Century Hermeneutics* (New Haven, Conn.: Yale Univ. Press, 1974); Sheehan, *Enlightenment Bible*.

7. For a fascinating account of the discipline of history's rise to independent, academic status (autonomous *Wissenschaft*), rather than its traditional role as a handmaiden of theology (*Hilfswissenschaft*), see Thomas Albert Howard, *Religion and the Rise of Historicism: W. M. L. de Wette, Jacob Burckhardt, and the Theological Origins of Nineteenth-Century Historical Consciousness* (Cambridge: Cambridge Univ. Press, 2000), 1 – 22.

8. Karl Barth, *Protestant Theology in the Nineteenth Century*, trans. B. Cozens and J. Bowden (Grand Rapids: Eerdmans, 2002), 476.

9. Quoted in Rudolf Smend, *From Astruc to Zimmerli: Old Testament Scholarship in Three Centuries*, trans. M. Kohl (Tübingen: Mohr Siebeck, 2007), 43.

Rational Mind, Romantic Impulse: The Formation of a Modern, Biblical Scholar

De Wette is a figure who straddled chronologically and, in many ways, intellectually the fence of the eighteenth and nineteenth centuries (1780 – 1849). De Wette was born on January 12, 1780, in Ulla, Germany, a city near Weimar.[10] His father, Johann Augustin (1744 – 1812), was a Lutheran pastor. Though there are few accounts of de Wette's youth, his childhood was healthy and happy. De Wette was the second of seven siblings and the firstborn son. His father played a formative role in his early education and eventual vocational choice.

De Wette entered the grammar school of Weimar in 1796. During this time, one could find within the city of Weimar such intellectuals as the poet Friedrich Schiller, author Johann Wolfgang Goethe, and philosopher Johann Gottfried Herder. De Wette's spare time in the evenings consisted of reading with friends the plays and philosophical writings of these figures.[11] He was a serious and respected student. A fellow student later described him as "an extremely gifted, earnest young man, who lived almost entirely for his studies and only rarely sought or needed social contacts. Through his sincere and successful industry and his calm and good behavior he earned the love of his teachers and the respect of his fellow students."[12]

De Wette's education was significantly shaped by Herder, the general superintendent of the Protestant Church and headmaster at the grammar school in Weimar. By the age of sixteen, de Wette had read Herder's *Ideas for the Philosophy of History of Humanity* and was taken with Herder's person and capacious intellect. As an adult, de Wette described his admiration for Herder:

> I still have a vivid impression of how I looked, with youthful admiration, at Herder's figure — a presence that was both kindly and inspired respect; how I listened to his sonorous voice and his solemnly formal words as he opened the public examination at the grammar school . . .

---

10. I have leaned heavily on John Rogerson's extensive research into the life and work of de Wette: *W. M. L. de Wette, Founder of Modern Biblical Criticism: An Intellectual Biography* (Sheffield: Sheffield Academic Press, 1991); idem, *Old Testament Criticism*. Also, Thomas Albert Howard's *Religion and the Rise of Historicism* has been especially important for this chapter.

11. Rogerson, *W. M. L. de Wette*, 15.

12. Ibid.

I can still see him standing in the pulpit, quiet and still, his hands one on top of the other, and I can still hear his unique monotone declaiming and expounding the Lord's Prayer in a reverent and profound manner.[13]

He later explained that Herder protected him from "the arid wastelands of theological criticism and rationalism" de Wette would encounter at the University of Jena.[14]

Herder's philosophical approach influenced de Wette's later biblical and theological work. There is a close connection between Herder and the history of religions school. Herder was a Romantic who rejected the Enlightenment devaluing of particulars in the search for the general or universal. Ideas and cultures are too intertwined for one to be isolated from the other. He also played a formative role in German philosophy's eventual "turn toward language."[15] For Herder, language is not a mere vehicle for describing the world (an overly formal and mechanistic view). Rather, language itself reveals a consciousness in humanity unique to particular people groups; it reveals their way of conceiving reality.[16] In other words, language reveals much about the people speaking. It is more than an inert mechanism ready-made to describe the world. We will turn to this matter more fully as we explore de Wette's work.[17] Suffice it to say, the Romanticist trajectory of Herder contributed much to the complex array of intellectual instincts in de Wette's work.

After a short stint as a Greek tutor for a young traveling Frenchman, de Wette entered university in Jena (1799). During de Wette's first year at Jena, he sat in on the lectures of famed New Testament scholar J. J. Griesbach (1745 – 1812).[18] Compared to other members of the faculty, Griesbach

---

13. Quoted in ibid., 16.

14. Howard, *Religion and the Rise of Historicism*, 26.

15. See Andrew Bowie, *Introduction to German Philosophy: From Kant to Habermas* (Cambridge: Polity, 2003) for a genetic account of the turn toward language that German idealism took.

16. Charles Taylor, *Hegel* (Cambridge: Cambridge Univ. Press, 1975), 19 – 20.

17. Herder will surface again in our engagement with Hermann Gunkel.

18. Griesbach — an early advocate of identifying New Testament manuscripts according to text families rather than allowing the majority of manuscripts a privileged status — is most remembered for his textual-critical work and his work on the "synoptic problem." Griesbach did much to champion a source-critical approach to Matthew, Mark, and Luke. He argued that Matthew wrote first, then Luke wrote his work by making use of Matthean material alongside other source material, and then Mark wrote his book as a conflation of both Matthew and Luke. Griesbach presented a synopsis of Matthew, Mark, and Luke not as an act of harmonization — a veritable tradition in the church, e.g., Augustine — but as a tool for comparison of the various sources. Because Griesbach did not

was probably a conservative. When viewed, however, against traditional notions of biblical inspiration, his critical approach to the "problems" of the Synoptic Gospels seemed radical.[19] This became an intellectual and spiritual problem for the young de Wette as he wrestled with the "contradictions" between the various gospel accounts of Jesus' life.

The intellectual and spiritual trials of the young de Wette can be seen in *Theodore*, a play he wrote in 1822, some twenty years after these events. Many of the elements of this play are autobiographical and reveal de Wette's understanding of his theological education.[20] De Wette writes about Theodore (a thinly veiled version of himself):

> The result of the theological studies of the first year was, in Theodore's case, that his former convictions concerning the origin of Christianity were shattered. The holy atmosphere of glory, which had hitherto surrounded the life of Jesus and the whole evangelical history, disappeared; but instead of a satisfactory historical insight, he had acquired only doubt, uncertainty, and incoherence of opinion.[21]

Faith and conviction were quickly unraveling for this Lutheran pastor's son and were being replaced with uncertainty and doubt.

Immanuel Kant's rationalism dominated the landscape of the University of Jena during this period. In his second year, de Wette attended the lectures of the deist Heinrich Paulus (1761 – 1851), as well as those of an unnamed Kantian philosopher of ethics.[22] The Kantian philosopher provided the certainty de Wette needed in the face of his theological doubt. Describing his fictional yet autobiographical Theodore, de Wette comments, "A whole new world was open to him; the thought of the independence of reason ... seized his mind with a mighty power."[23] The shackles of dogmatism were rattling at his feet as he moved toward the independence of reason. Thomas Howard articulates the kind of transformation taking

---

allow John's gospel into the schema, the term "Synoptic Gospels" became standard fare in scholarly discourse referring to the first three of the fourfold gospel. See Stephen Neill and Tom Wright, *The Interpretation of the New Testament, 1861 – 1986* (The Firth Lectures; New York: Oxford Univ. Press, 1988), 72 – 73.

19. See Donald K. McKim, ed., *Dictionary of Major Biblical Interpreters* (Downers Grove, Ill.: InterVarsity, 2007), 492.

20. On the significance of *Theodore* for giving an account of de Wette's own intellectual biography, see Howard, *Religion and the Rise of Historicism*, 29 – 32; Rogerson, *W. M. L. de Wette*.

21. Quoted in Howard, *Religion and the Rise of Historicism*, 30.

22. See Rogerson, *W. M. L. de Wette*, 31.

23. Quoted in Howard, *Religion and the Rise of Historicism*, 31.

place in de Wette, "He learned to translate the doctrines of his youth — conversion, rebirth, grace, the love of God and Christ, and so on — into Kantian philosophical categories."[24] Kant's differentiating of the timeless truths of reason from the historically conditioned form of ecclesial and biblical knowledge became paradigmatic for biblical criticism of this period. The seeds sown by Spinoza are now in full bloom. Timeless truths of reason located in the categories of the mind now recoil from the historically particular Bible of a more primitive and less sophisticated period of human history.

De Wette was too complex a thinker and feeler for such bald rationalism. He soon became dissatisfied with this approach. Herder's romantic impulses were too embedded in de Wette and would not allow him to accept whole hog Kant's epistemology or ethics. Kant's religion leaves one only with morality, resulting in an absence of beauty and feeling (e.g., aesthetics). De Wette writes of Theodore, "The Kantian doctrine of God which reason enjoined, namely, that the rule of virtue should be established in the world and should be rewarded with good fortune, this fell like a damp squib into his soul, extinguishing the holy fire of devotion and leaving in its place a dismal darkness."[25] In de Wette's earliest writing, *An Idea Concerning the Study of Religion* (1801), he describes the deleterious effects of this Kantian religion, a religion "devoid of nourishment for the spirit and heart."[26] The intellectual and religious situation of the young de Wette was now quite complex. On the one hand, Kant's influence was such that he would never return to the simplicity of his childhood faith. On the other hand, Kant's rationalism did not fill the aesthetic and religious void that de Wette so desperately felt.[27]

Friedrich Wilhelm Joseph Schelling's lectures on the philosophy of art proved important for the young de Wette.[28] Schelling taught that the world and all of its modes of thought emanate from the Absolute (i.e., God).[29] Therefore, even the Kantian rationalism so dominant during that day was

---

24. Ibid.

25. Quoted in Rogerson, *W. M. L. de Wette*, 31.

26. *Eine Idee über das Studium der Theologie.* Quoted in Howard, *Religion and the Rise of Historicism*, 31.

27. See Rogerson, *W. M. L. de Wette*, 36 – 38.

28. On Schelling's philosophy of nature and art, see Bowie, *Introduction to German Philosophy*, 71 – 78.

29. See F. W. J. Schelling, *Philosophy and Religion*, trans. K. Ottmann (New York: Spring Publications, 2010).

itself only a part of the Absolute and could not account for the whole of reality (as important as the analytical skills it offered were). Even the Bible with all its myth and supernatural elements was not an embarrassment to modern humanity.[30] Neither was the Bible to be stripped down to mere morality because the Bible itself was a part of the Absolute as well. In this sense, the Bible was worthy of respect and study as a religious expression of a people striving for the Absolute.[31]

Schelling viewed art and aesthetics as the pinnacle of human reason because the creation of the world itself was the act of divine imagination. Reason alone could not account for the aesthetics present in the world around us. This turn toward aesthetics touched a nerve in de Wette. Even though the supernatural faith of his childhood had been irremediably displaced by Kant's philosophy, de Wette stated, "My feelings rebelled loudly against the conviction of my reason."[32] The turn toward aesthetics and art now became the sphere for engaging the divine "since there is no longer a Christ on earth who can teach us to know the heavenly Father."[33]

It is worth quoting in full de Wette's account of this "conversion" in his *Idea Concerning the Study of Religion*:

> An unforgettable outward circumstance occasioned the happiest revolution in my inner life and gave me back the peace I had lost. The imperfect, cloudy faith of my childhood was replaced by one higher and better, the remembrance of God awoke in my heart to new life, and belief in immortality returned in a higher, transformed form. Now theology was for me no longer cold, grim moral censor, nor even merely a daughter of history; it increasingly rose up before my eyes to higher, heavenly majesty, to divine dignity.[34]

A high esteem for aesthetics, the importance of religious feeling, and the necessary role "myth" plays in shaping and ordering our world left an indelible stamp on de Wette's approach to the Old Testament. In time, the category of myth would become central to his understanding of the Old Testament. Moreover, an appreciation for myth created in de Wette a deep

---

30. Commenting on Schelling's understanding of myth, Rogerson states, "Thus, mythology was not the attempt of crude natives to understand the world of nature; it was a necessary form of religion in which an admittedly incomplete attempt was made to grasp the Absolute" (*W. M. L. de Wette*, 34).

31. See Howard, *Religion and the Rise of Historicism*, 32–33.

32. Quoted in Smend, *From Astruc to Zimmerli*, 46.

33. Ibid.

34. Ibid.

enthusiasm for the Bible: "Welcome, holy record of the primal world, rich treasure of the good and the beautiful, book of books! How will I feed on thee, how will I enrich myself from thy abundance!"[35] In due course, I will return more fully to de Wette's understanding of myth and the influence of the "mythical school" on his critical engagement of the Old Testament. It is important to observe here the confluence of rationalistic, romantic, and mythical instincts in de Wette's religious thought.

De Wette's years at the University of Jena were highly productive. In September 1804, de Wette submitted his doctoral dissertation, *A Critical-Exegetical Dissertation by which Deuteronomy, Different from the Earlier Books of the Pentateuch, Is Shown to Be the Work of a Later Author*, a work only sixteen pages in length.[36] A sixteen-page dissertation is shockingly short by today's standards. The work was measured by its quality, however, and not its length.[37] Within this work, the seeds of critical insight were sown that would eventually shape Pentateuchal studies — e.g., that Deuteronomy was written later than the other books of the Pentateuch. In a long footnote, de Wette made an offhanded remark that Deuteronomy or some form of it may have been the law book discovered by Josiah in 622 BC. In time, this theory would become standard fare. De Wette's dissertation earned him a doctorate in March 1805. Most likely by the fall of 1805, he was a *Privatdozent* (unpaid university lecturer) at Jena.

De Wette's most significant writing during his time at Jena, and unquestionably the most significant Old Testament work of this period, was his two-volume *Contributions to the Introduction of the Old Testament*.[38] These two volumes appeared in 1806–1807 and developed a thesis regarding Israelite religion and literary history that has shaped the critical studies of the Old Testament to this day. We will engage these volumes more substantially in the next section of this chapter. De Wette also wrote *An Invitation to the Study of the Hebrew Language and Literature* in 1805 to mark the beginning of his lectureship at Jena. In this work, de Wette complained that the study of the Hebrew language and literature was not

---

35. Ibid., 47.

36. *Dissertatio Critico-Exegetica qua a prioribus Deuteronomium pentateuchi libris diversum, alius cuiusdam recentioris auctoris opus esse monstratur.*

37. German dissertations even of a generation ago could be markedly shorter than the standard 80,000- to 100,000-word dissertations of today.

38. Wilhelm Martin Leberecht de Wette, *Beiträge zur Einleitung in das Alte Testament*, 2 vols. (Hildesheim, Germany: G. Olms, 1971).

being taken seriously enough in the academy.[39] The publication of these works reveals the prodigious nature of de Wette's scholarly production during his Jena days.

There is a tragic element to de Wette's Jena days. Shortly after receiving the doctorate, he married Eberhardine Boye, who then died in childbirth ten months after their wedding. Rudolf Smend describes de Wette's suffering:

> The marriage lasted barely a year, until the beginning of 1806; then his wife, who was five years older than himself, died, following the birth of a still-born child. The happiness of that year remained with him all his life; he never found it again in two later marriages. In addition, in October of 1806 he lost everything he possessed in the looting which followed the French victories at the battles of Jena and Auerstedt.[40]

One can only imagine the toll such cascading events took in de Wette's life. As a broken man, de Wette accepted an invitation to a chair in 1807 at the University of Heidelberg. De Wette only spent three years there. The bulk of his scholarly efforts during these days was translation work.[41] Commentaries on the biblical books were supposed to accompany these translations, but only one commentary saw the light of day. The commentary that appeared was on the Psalms (published in 1811 but researched and written mostly during his tenure at Heidelberg). De Wette's Psalms commentary anticipated by almost a century many of Gunkel's form-critical analyses of the Psalter, which we will discuss in chapter 4.

De Wette later complained by letter to Friedrich Schleiermacher that he had been teaching fifteen to seventeen hours a week on the Old and New Testaments to a group of hearers he increasingly found unseemly. De Wette described them as "half barbarians and cheats."[42] Happily then, in 1810, de Wette accepted an invitation from Schleiermacher for a chair on the theology faculty of the newly formed university in Berlin.[43]

De Wette's tenure in Berlin was marked by academic activity and achievement of the highest order. In 1813 and 1815, he published two

---

39. See Rogerson, *W. M. L. de Wette*, 45.

40. Smend, *From Astruc to Zimmerli*, 50.

41. For details on de Wette's work during his time in Heidelberg, see Rogerson, *W. M. L. de Wette*, chapter 3.

42. Rogerson, *W. M. L. de Wette*, 84.

43. See ibid.; Howard, *Religion and the Rise of Historicism*, 50.

volumes of dogmatic/historical theology.[44] In 1815, he published a commentary on his dogmatics titled *Concerning Religion and Theology*.[45] He wrote a book on Hebrew-Jewish archaeology in 1814; and in 1817, he wrote his *Introduction to the Old Testament*. A book on the synopsis of the gospels appeared in 1818, and between 1819–1823, de Wette's multivolume work on Christian ethics was published.[46] De Wette was also a founding editor of the *Theologische Zeitschrift* (Theological Journal), along with his colleagues Schleiermacher and Friedrich Lücke.[47]

The relationship between de Wette and Schleiermacher initially was, in the words of Smend, "somewhat cool, if not strained."[48] De Wette's melancholic personality and cool detachment was not well received by the students. On the other hand, Schleiermacher's brilliance and effervescence were praised. Those who are involved in the academy to this day understand how such student sentiments can cause friction between various faculty members, despite their theological agreement. Smend's account of this relationship relays the reconciling role Lücke played. Lücke took de Wette to hear Schleiermacher preach. When de Wette heard Schleiermacher preach, he recognized that he and Schleiermacher were indeed compatible as colleagues and friends. As time passed, de Wette became close with the Schleiermacher family. He was godfather to Schleiermacher's only son, Nathaniel, who died at the young age of nine.[49]

De Wette's academic career at Berlin, brilliant though it was, came to an abrupt halt. Due to a political tightening of the screws under the minister of education in Berlin, de Wette was dismissed from his post at the university in 1819. A student named Karl Ludwig Sand had murdered a well-known German playwright. The student unions believed the playwright to be a traitor and Russian loyalist. These student unions viewed Sand's murdering of this man as an act of devotion to the motherland. The Prussian authorities of the time did not agree. Full-fledged investigations took place after the murder, and particular attention was given to university professors and their influence on the young. De Wette actually knew

---

44. *Lehrbuch der christlichen Dogmatik in ihrer historischen Entwicklung dargestellt*, 2 vols., 3rd ed. (Berlin: G. Reimer, 1831).

45. *Über Religion und Theologie* (Berlin: Realschulbuchhandlung, 1815).

46. *Christliche Sittenlehre*, 3 vols. (Berlin: G. Reimer, 1819–23).

47. See Smend, *From Astruc to Zimmerli*, 50–51.

48. Ibid., 51.

49. Ibid.

Sand and had written a letter of condolence to his mother after Sand was killed. Though de Wette disagreed with the murder, he described Sand as a devout person of virtue.[50] Such sentiments put de Wette at odds with the authorities, and he was dismissed from his post. Another significant tragedy now marked de Wette's academic life.

After a brief period as pastor of St. Catherine's Church in Brunswick, de Wette accepted an appointment at the University of Basel in 1822. According to Smend's account, de Wette accepted the chair with a heavy heart.[51] Pietists within the city of Berlin opposed his appointment. Smend observes, "When he arrived in Basel, a Pietist remarked that now the Devil had built a chapel next to the house of the Lord (the Basel mission)."[52] Though his interest in the Old Testament continued, de Wette's primary work in Basel was his *Brief Exegetical Handbook to the New Testament*, a commentary on all the New Testament writings.

De Wette spent over twenty years on the faculty at the University of Basel. Rogerson describes the ending of de Wette's academic career in Basel: "On 31 May 1847, a torchlight procession, the like of which had not been seen for many years, ended the celebrations in Basel which honoured twenty-five years of work as professor of theology by Wilhelm Martin Leberecht de Wette."[53] De Wette invested a great deal of energy into the university and did much to guarantee the international reputation of its theology faculty. When he died on June 16, 1849, he died a Swiss citizen and a Reformed clergyman.

De Wette died in a theological no-man's-land. He was much too left of center for the orthodox, those who had a high regard for the church's creeds and the inspiration and authority of Scripture. And he was too right of center for the rationalists of the day, who discounted all things religious. De Wette was a man caught, and perhaps in hindsight, lost in the middle.

Romanticism and Historicism: De Wette's Historical Approach to the Old Testament

The legacy and name of de Wette are primarily preserved today by Old Testament scholars. The book you are reading is a case in point. Unfortunately,

---

50. Ibid., 53; see Rogerson, *W. M. L. de Wette*, 148–59.
51. Smend, *From Astruc to Zimmerli*, 54–55.
52. Ibid., 55.
53. Rogerson, *W. M. L. de Wette*, 13.

this is a limited appreciation of the scope and significance of his work. Many theologians have puzzled over de Wette's fading into theological obscurity. As I mentioned in the introduction, Karl Barth wondered if under differing historical circumstances de Wette would have eclipsed Schleiermacher as the great theologian of the nineteenth century.[54] Speculations aside, it must be understood that the scope of de Wette's work went beyond the Old Testament. De Wette was a theologian of the first order who wrote works on Old Testament, New Testament, Christian dogmatics, Christian ethics, and even dramatic plays. His literary output was an enormous achievement, and it does not do de Wette justice that we focus only on his Old Testament work. Nevertheless, the aims and intentions of this volume demand this limitation.[55]

De Wette's straddling of theological and philosophical worlds created difficult tensions. For in de Wette, one finds an aesthetic, a mystic, and a rationalist all rolled into one.[56] More specifically, de Wette was both a romanticist and a historicist.[57] These two impulses within de Wette influenced his approach to the critical study of the Old Testament. De Wette's particular approach to historical matters within the Scriptures was not to gain factual knowledge of Israel's empirical history per se. De Wette was not interested in the events of Scripture "as they really happened" because Israel's Scriptures were not written to give that kind of historical factuality. The investigation of Israel's history is a discrete discipline, a different realm of knowledge, from the examination of the literary content of Israel's sacred texts. According to de Wette, one should not collapse disciplines distinct from one another.

Howard describes de Wette as one who accepted the tensions between faith and reason to such an extent that he never tried to show the comparability of the two like Schleiermacher did.[58] De Wette allowed the tensions to remain. An example of this can be seen in de Wette's approach to the book of Chronicles. For a rationalist understanding of history (eventually seen in its fullness with logical positivism, an approach to history that works strictly within the framework of verifiability or the lack thereof) the

---

54. See Barth, *Protestant Theology*, 476.

55. For a fuller description of de Wette's work as a whole, see Rogerson, *W. M. L. de Wette*.

56. See "De Wette," in *Dictionary of Biblical Interpretation*, ed. John H. Hayes (Nashville: Abingdon, 1999), 1:294.

57. See Howard, *Religion and the Rise of Historicism*, 24.

58. Ibid., 107.

matter is either/or. Either the events the book of Chronicles relays happened, or they did not. If they did not, then Chronicles as a literary work is deemed fraudulent.[59]

But for de Wette, the matter was not either/or; it was both/and. As will be seen, de Wette did deny the historical veracity of much of the Pentateuch and Chronicles (historical veracity having to do with the historical events described in these books). Commenting on the critical problems of Chronicles, Brevard Childs states:

> The major credit for breaking open the exegetical problems of Chronicles in its most radical and challenging form goes to de Wette in his *Beiträge* (1807). De Wette argued that the writer "reworked, altered, and falsified" his earlier sources in the interest of a tendentious dogmatic frame of reference so as to render it useless as a historical source.[60]

As can be seen, de Wette concurs with a rational historical account of Chronicles, namely, Chronicles is of no value as a historical source. It did not follow for de Wette, however, that Chronicles is then falsified as a religious document or as a certain kind of historical document. Instead of relaying faithfully the events attested in these documents, we have before us a text describing the religious-historical outlook, worldview, and feelings of the authors who wrote these works. The type of historical investigation de Wette engages in is one or two steps removed from the events themselves attested in the biblical literature.[61] A different type of historical investigation emerges with de Wette.

This new approach to history, it can be argued, is de Wette's enduring legacy on the critical study of the Old Testament. The type of history one is dealing with in the Old Testament is "religious history." In this sense, the Scriptures have become religion as they attest to the religious impulses found within the history of Israel's encounter with her God. De Wette's approach to the critical study of the Old Testament is surely "historical-critical." At the same time, it is an approach not as interested in

---

59. See Howard on how de Wette and David Friedrich Strauss differed here regarding the life of Jesus (*Religion and the Rise of Historicism*, 106 – 8).

60. Brevard S. Childs, *Introduction to the Old Testament as Scripture* (Philadelphia: Fortress, 1979), 642.

61. Here de Wette departs from the historical-critical approach of J. G. Eichhorn, who focused on the recovery of the literary sources that lie behind the Pentateuch in an effort to safeguard the veracity of the biblical traditions (see John Van Seters, *The Edited Bible: The Curious History of the "Editor" in Biblical Criticism* (Winona Lake, Ind.: Eisenbrauns, 2006), 207 – 8).

the events as they really occurred (a historically conditioned "behind the text" approach). Rather, his historical investigation was one step removed from "the events in themselves." For de Wette, the relaying of these anti-quated events in the particularities of Israel's religious history tells us some-thing about these particular people and their religious expressions and sentiments. This is especially true of de Wette's approach to the Pentateuch, namely, that the Pentateuch and its various literary strata have more to tell us about the time of Israel's monarchy than about Israel's genetic history.

The influence of Herder and Schelling on de Wette is poignant here. The particularity of historical peoples, cultures, and their languages was valued by these thinkers because metaphysical truths are always culturally conditioned in their reception. The search for universal forms of reason tends to run roughshod over the aesthetic and cultural aspects of human thinking and being. This is also the case for the engagement of the Old Testament. Israel's religious expression and sentiment are valuable and worthy of investigation in their own right and not merely as a vehicle for abstract principles of morality (as in Kant). Because of this aesthetic, romantic instinct in de Wette, myth has a positive and major role to play in understanding Israel's religious history and literature.

De Wette was influenced by the "mythical school" consisting of J. G. Eichhorn, J. B. Gabler, and G. L. Bauer.[62] Like Herder, Eichhorn resisted the Enlightenment instinct to flatten out time and cultures with an appeal to universal truths of reason. For Eichhorn, the Old Testament texts were the product of a different culture, and exegesis of these texts demanded sen-sitivity to this dynamic (even if the culture did have a "primitive mind").[63] Part and parcel of this cultural appreciation involved a recognition of

---

62. Gabler is most remembered for his 1787 address titled "On the Proper Distinction Between Biblical and Dogmatic Theology and the Specific Objectives of Each." It is fair to say that Gabler's title has been more influential than the actual content of his address. It was used later, especially in the 1800s, as a defense of the strict separation of biblical theology and dogmatics. Gabler's address is not calling for the strict separation of dogmatics from biblical theology. Rather, it sought to pro-vide an historically informed foundation from which dogmatics could operate. Once one examined historically what the various biblical authors were saying in their particular books (*Auslegung* [*inter-pretation*]), then one extrapolated from these various particular authors the abstract principles they held in common (*Erklärung* [*explanation*]). What one is left with during this abstracting process he called a "pure biblical theology" (*reine biblische Theologie*). See Mark Elliott, "Gabler, Johann Philipp," in *Dictionary of Major Biblical Interpreters*, 452 – 56; Brevard S. Childs, *Biblical Theology of the Old and New Testaments: Theological Reflection on the Christian Bible* (Minneapolis: Fortress, 1992), 4 – 6; Magne Saebø, *On the Way to Canon: Creative Tradition History in the Old Testament* (Journal for the Study of the Old Testament; Sheffield: Sheffield Academic Press, 1998), 310 – 26.

63. Howard, *Religion and the Rise of Historicism*, 37.

Israel's "historical" documents as a mixture of historical and mythical elements. Though their objectives may have differed, the mythical school of Eichhorn and Gabler recognized their task as separating the mythical from the historical and giving those mythical elements a more naturalistic explanation. The mythical in the Old Testament are those stories, legends, or tales that do not stand up to the critical scrutiny of an enlightened mind.[64] Tales such as the creation narratives or Lot's wife turning into salt were given a more natural explanation for what really happened behind those mythically relayed events. By way of example, Rogerson states, "What lay behind Genesis 2 – 3 was the experience of a human couple who had become aware of their sexual differences as the result of eating slightly poisonous fruit from a tree."[65] The mythical portions of the Old Testament were the only way the ancient Israelite knew how to express such matters and were indicative of their primitive minds.[66] "De-mythologization" in this early form became a constituent aspect of historical-critical engagement with the Old Testament texts.

De Wette's critical engagement of the Old Testament owed much to the groundwork laid by the mythical school. At the same time, de Wette differed from the mystical school in significant ways. First, de Wette did not make it his goal to differentiate the mythical from the historical in order to establish the latter. De Wette had a dubious outlook on the historical character of all the historical books in the Bible. He also did not believe the biblical authors should be conceived of as historians.[67] "The Hebrew storyteller is not a historian in an actual sense; he is a prophet and seer looking into the past," writes de Wette.[68] For de Wette, the historical character of the Old Testament has to do with the religious makeup of the various authors and redactors actually composing or compiling the material; it is not historical in any sense of reporting the events as they actually occurred.

Second, and following from the first, de Wette had a very high view of

---

64. Ibid., 36 – 37.

65. Rogerson, *Old Testament Criticism*, 18.

66. Ibid., 18. Howard points out that the mythical school did not "scoff" at the Old Testament because of these mythical elements (*Religion and the Rise of Historicism*, 37). This is especially true of Gabler's more "faithful" approach to these matters as an apologetic defense of the Old Testament against derision from the intellectual elites of the day. See John Rogerson, "Eichhorn, J. G.," in *Dictionary of Major Biblical Interpreters*, 401.

67. See Howard, *Religion and the Rise of Historicism*, 38.

68. Quoted in ibid.

myth and did not see it as something needing to be expunged from the Old Testament. For it is within the mythic traditions of the ancient Israelites that one gains access to their religious outlook and feelings. Here, again, Herder's influence can be observed. The culture and customs of a people are animated by their own *Volkgeist* (spirit of the people).[69] Gaining access to the spirit of the people does not entail a dismissal of their folklore and customs. Rather, one must embrace these as carrying within them an explanatory function of who and what these ancient peoples were. De Wette's historicism and rationalism merge together in his approach to the literature and history of the Old Testament people. The historical documents of the Old Testament tell us relatively little about the events they relay. They do, however, tell us much about the religious outlook, feeling, and beliefs of those who composed the documents and cherished them as their sacred writings.

Biblical criticism of the Old Testament, for de Wette, is not an attempt to arrive at the events as they really occurred. Biblical criticism is an engagement of the mythical character of Israel's religious documents for the purpose of gaining insight into Israel's own religious beliefs. By way of illustration, no one thinks Virgil's *Aeneid* gives us an accurate account of Rome's historical genesis. The *Aeneid* does, however, tell us much about ancient Rome in the time of Octavian and his rise to power as Caesar Augustus. De Wette approaches the historical materials of the Old Testament in a similar fashion. As a historical document relaying events as they occurred in time and space, it is of little value. As a document that reveals the historically conditioned religious feeling and expression of ancient Israel, it is a treasure trove of pertinent information.

De Wette's *Contributions*

Our attention turns now to an outline of his major insights in his most important work, *Contributions to the Introduction of the Old Testament*. De Wette's publication of *Contributions* (*Beiträge*) marked a watershed event in the history of Old Testament interpretation. Rogerson describes de Wette's Old Testament scholarship as the initiation of "a new era" in the discipline.[70] This does not mean that de Wette's critical insights had

---

69. Louis Dupré, *The Enlightenment and the Intellectual Foundations of Modern Culture* (New Haven, Conn.: Yale Univ. Press, 2004), 220.

70. Rogerson, *Old Testament Criticism*, 28; see also Van Seters, *Edited Bible*, 205.

no precursors. For example, J. S. Vater's *Commentary on the Pentateuch* (1802 – 1805) played a role in de Wette's thought, as well as Eichhorn's seminal insights on the lateness of Chronicles.[71] Nevertheless, de Wette's penetrating analysis and categories have had a lasting impact on the critical interpretation of the Old Testament.

De Wette's *Contributions* is a two-volumed work, with the claims of the second volume following logically from the conclusions of the first. In the first volume, de Wette addresses specifically the compositional history of the book of Chronicles. De Wette challenged Eichhorn's assumption that Chronicles depended on the same ancient source used in the composition of Samuel and Kings. The evidence for Eichhorn's claim was too thin and did not provide a satisfactory answer for the problems created by such a theory, namely, the large amount of material not shared between the books of Samuel/Kings and Chronicles. De Wette's novel claim was that Chronicles depended on Samuel/Kings in its compositional history. The divergence in the material suggests both a late date and different religious-historical setting from the compiler of the Samuel/Kings material.

Moreover, de Wette denies that Chronicles can be used with any confidence as a historical record of Israel's preexilic history. The book of Chronicles attests to the theological and religious outlook of the postexilic community as it construed the preexilic period along Pentateuchal lines of thought. The book of Kings deals with both Israel and Judah in the divided monarchy, giving attention to both realms of the divided kingdom, whereas Chronicles is slow to speak of the northern kingdom. Again, this reveals Chronicles' postexilic setting and preoccupation with Judah.[72]

De Wette spends much exegetical energy showing the divergences between Samuel/Kings and its relationship to the worshiping practices of the Pentateuch and Chronicles. In the latter, a full-blown cultic experience is taking place in postexilic Israel: the sanctuary is repaired in Jerusalem; there is a precise understanding of how sacrifices are to be made, and the Levitical priesthood is active.[73] One searches in vain, according to de Wette, for such Pentateuchal cultic realities in any sedimented form in the earlier Samuel/Kings material. What this shows, most importantly, is that the earlier sources of Samuel/Kings did not know about the specifics

---

71. See Smend, *From Astruc to Zimmerli*, 49; Rogerson, *Old Testament Criticism*, 28 – 30.
72. De Wette, *Beiträge*, 1:126 – 32.
73. Ibid., 1:80 – 102.

of the Pentateuchal cultic system, as the postexilic religious community did. Why did they not know? Because they were not yet fully in existence.

Here a crucial interpretive move is made, whose implications will be worked out more fully with Julius Wellhausen. The Pentateuch, along with the Torah and its cultic instructions, is, according to de Wette, actually the product of the monarchical period of Israel's history. It was not antecedent to the time of Israel's kings in their empirical history, even though the canonical presentation of Israel's history presents it as such. Rogerson states, "Much attention is paid to the account of the discovery of the Book of the Law in the reign of Josiah (2 Kings 22), with de Wette insisting that it was the discovery of something *that had not been previously known.*"[74] The book of Chronicles' portrayal of the early kings of Israel as fully involved in an established cultic practice is an anachronistic rereading of Israel's history along ideological and theological lines. This would be similar to seeing a Renaissance painting of the soldiers at Jesus' tomb dressed not in Roman garb but in costumes looking very much like Ponce de Leon. One looks at such a painting and intuitively knows that something is not quite right. This is how de Wette understands Chronicles. The events as they are attested in Chronicles are falsified historically. At the same time, however, the narration of those events is extremely important as one comes to grips with the religious-historical outlook of the postexilic community of Judah. It is along these interpretive lines that Chronicles needs to be read.

As mentioned above, de Wette's second volume follows from the first. If the early monarchy of Israel did not in fact have an established cult, centralized place of worship, and Levitical priesthood, what then does this say about the Pentateuch? As argued by others before, the Pentateuch was not authored by Moses in the time of Israel's exodus from Egypt. Rather, Genesis-Numbers were mythical documents that tell us more about the religious outlook of Israel's early monarchy in the tenth century than they do about the history of Israel's beginnings. Again, this is an epic account of Genesis-Numbers that compares to Virgil's *Aeneid* and the history of Rome.

Deuteronomy, as argued in de Wette's dissertation, is later than the rest of the Pentateuch, probably postexilic in its final form. For de Wette, some of the material in Deuteronomy is contained in the documents discovered by Josiah, but only in fragment form. Eventually these fragments

---

74. Rogerson, *Old Testament Criticism*, 31; see de Wette, *Beiträge*, 1:175–77.

grew and developed into the final form of the book that we now have in the postexilic period.[75]

Rogerson helpfully summarizes the main points of de Wette's *Contributions*. I will paraphrase them as follows:

1. Chronicles is late in composition; it reveals the religion of Israel in the postexilic period.

2. The Pentateuch as a whole is a late compilation.

3. The traditions recounted in the Pentateuch provide no reliable information about the empirical history and genesis of Israel in its presettlement days. These materials are mythical and not historical.

4. The actual history of Israel and the narrated history of Israel are quite different from one another. The formation of the cult, the centrality of the Torah, and the establishment of the Levitical priesthood are all late developments in Israel's religious history, even though the religious documents of the Old Testament recount a different tale.[76]

It is important to remember that for de Wette, his account of Israel's religious history and mythical understanding of Israel's historical documents did not contain a negative appraisal meant to falsify the Bible as a religious document. For de Wette, as well as his Berlin colleague Schleiermacher, to study *theology* is to study *religion*. To study religion is to enter into a romantic appreciation of various groups' feelings and sense of the divine. Such is the case with Old Testament studies as well. Though the Bible's historical veracity comes out looking poorly, Israel's history of religion does not. Or, at least, so de Wette thought.

Conclusion

Much more could and should be said about de Wette.[77] The study of the Old Testament after de Wette would never be the same. The historical critical study of the Old Testament is henceforth identified primarily as an engagement with Israel's history of religion. A major division between the canonical history of Israel and the empirical history of Israel is established.

---

75. See Rogerson, *Old Testament Criticism*, 34.

76. Ibid.

77. For example, de Wette's indebtedness to the philosophical scheme of J. F. Fries (see Rogerson, *Old Testament Criticism*, 44–49; Howard, *Religion and the Rise of Historicism*, 43–50).

The text of the Old Testament is no longer a continuing *witness* of divine revelation but is now a *source* for the critical retrieval of Israel's religious history. Or in other terms, the study of the Bible became the historically conditioned study of ancient Israel's religion.

FOR FURTHER READING

Barth, Karl. *Protestant Theology in the Nineteenth Century.* Translated by B. Cozens and J. Bowden. Grand Rapids: Eerdmans, 2002.

Bowie, Andrew. *Introduction to German Philosophy: From Kant to Habermas.* Cambridge, UK: Polity, 2003.

De Wette, Wilhelm Martin Leberecht. *Beiträge zur Einleitung in das Alte Testament.* 2 vols. Hildesheim, Germany: G. Olms, 1971.

Dupré, Louis. *The Enlightenment and the Intellectual Foundations of Modern Culture.* New Haven, Conn.: Yale Univ. Press, 2004.

Frei, Hans. *The Eclipse of Biblical Narrative: A Study in Eighteenth and Nineteenth Century Hermeneutics.* New Haven, Conn.: Yale Univ. Press, 1974.

Howard, Thomas Albert. *Religion and the Rise of Historicism: W. M. L. de Wette, Jacob Burckhardt, and the Theological Origins of Nineteenth-Century Historical Consciousness.* Cambridge: Cambridge Univ. Press, 2000.

Legaspi, Michael C. *The Death of Scripture and the Rise of Biblical Studies.* Oxford Studies in Historical Theology. New York: Oxford Univ. Press, 2010.

O'Neill, J. C. *The Bible's Authority: A Portrait Gallery of Thinkers from Lessing to Bultmann.* Edinburgh: T&T Clark, 1991.

Rogerson, John. *Old Testament Criticism in the Nineteenth Century: England and Germany.* Minneapolis: Fortress, 1985.

———. *W. M. L. de Wette, Founder of Modern Biblical Criticism: An Intellectual Biography.* Sheffield: Sheffield Academic Press, 1991.

Smend, Rudolf. *From Astruc to Zimmerli: Old Testament Scholarship in Three Centuries.* Translated by M. Kohl. Tübingen: Mohr Siebeck, 2007.

Van Seters, John. *The Edited Bible: The Curious History of the "Editor" in Biblical Criticism.* Winona Lake, Ind.: Eisenbrauns, 2006.

Julius Wellhausen

(1844–1918)

Israel's History and Literary Sources

THE NAME JULIUS WELLHAUSEN LOOMS LARGE IN ANY ACCOUNT OF modern criticism. His position in the history of Old Testament interpretation is much like a great divide between a before and an after. Like all within the history of ideas, Wellhausen's Old Testament interpretation did not take place in isolation from figures who preceded him. Johann Salomo Semler, Wilhelm Vatke, Abraham Kuenen, Heinrich Ewald, and Karl H. Graf, to name a few, provided Wellhausen with the critical tools needed for his own work. For example, Wellhausen was not the first to notice sources in the Pentateuch. Such an enterprise began over a century before Wellhausen with the work of Jean Astruc (1684–1766) and Richard Simon (1638–1712). Neither was Wellhausen the first to suggest that the prophets of Israel came before the law of Moses. Graf suggested this seminal idea, and Wellhausen seized the notion when he first heard it. Nevertheless, it is Wellhausen's name that towers above these figures for his clarity and the broad scope of his project, namely, a new conception of Israel's history.

Country Roots, University Professor, and a New History of Israel

A definitive biography of Julius Wellhausen has not been written, due in part to the fact that he never had children. Adding to this difficulty was the destruction of all of his personal manuscripts and letters by his widowed wife, though some seven hundred letters still exist in various publications and private collections.[1] Rudolf Smend is able to offer one of the better accounts of Wellhausen the man. Smend's grandfather was Wellhausen's closest friend, his father and siblings growing up under the eye of Wellhausen. When Smend wrote an article in 1982 on Wellhausen's life and work, he still had a living uncle who used to swim with Wellhausen on the river Leine. This uncle denied the rumor that Wellhausen preferred to swim on Sunday morning so the pious churchgoers could see him with a bathing suit over his shoulder. While the rumor may be false, the tension between Wellhausen and the church was not.

Wellhausen was born on May 17, 1844, in Hameln, Germany. Hameln is the town of the famed Pied Piper, an analogy not lost on Wellhausen's orthodox detractors. His father, August Wellhausen, was a Lutheran pastor in the small rural town. Wellhausen always viewed himself more a man of the country than the city. He told his colleague Albert Socin that "he would rather be a country squire instead of a university professor."[2] This rural setting gave Wellhausen an eye for the particular, and his academic approach has been described as "straightforward."[3] A no-nonsense, non-pretentious quality often associated with rural farmer types is displayed in Wellhausen's work — "snobbery was foreign to him."[4] Life in Hameln shaped Wellhausen in this way.

His father was a cultured and learned man — Wellhausen remembered his father as the only man in the neighborhood with a copy of Goethe's work.[5] August Wellhausen was also a high church, confessional Lutheran whose strong liturgical interests set his theological outlook over against the rising theological liberalism of the day. By all accounts, Wellhausen's early childhood in Hameln was happy. This is quite remarkable, given the constant barrage of physical ailments on his family. His father was neuropathic and incapable of work for periods of time. He died at the age of fifty-two.[6] The hearing problems of Wellhausen's mother's eventually led to her complete deafness. Of the four children, Julius was the only son

---

1. Rudolf Smend, "Julius Wellhausen and His *Prolegomena to the History of Israel*," *Semeia* 25 (1982): 4.
2. Quoted in Bernhard Maier, *William Robertson Smith: His Life, His Work and His Times* (Forschungen zum Alten Testament; Tübingen: Mohr Siebeck, 2009), 49.
3. Smend, "Wellhausen and His *Prolegomena*," 5.
4. Rudolf Smend, *From Astruc to Zimmerli: Old Testament Scholarship in Three Centuries*, trans. M. Kohl (Tübingen: Mohr Siebeck, 2007), 91.
5. Ibid.
6. Ibid.

to outlive his parents. Wellhausen himself "was continually plagued by insomnia, had gastric trouble, was as good as deaf before he was sixty, and years before his death was prevented from any kind of work by arteriosclerosis."[7] Despite these difficulties, Wellhausen was well-adjusted and of sound mental health.

Though Wellhausen did not follow in his father's orthodox footprints — recognizing the toll this rejection took on his family, Wellhausen later confessed, "I was only sorry for my mother" — he did begin the study of theology at the University of Göttingen in 1862. He had a special affinity for the narratives of the Old Testament (the stories of Saul, David, Ahab, and Elijah were particular favorites), the hymns of the church, and the piety of several examples from the Middle Ages.[8] But Wellhausen did not think these modest interests warranted academic theological studies. The situation changed, however, during the Easter break of 1863 when Wellhausen happened upon a book by Heinrich Ewald (1803 – 1875) on the history of Israel. Wellhausen was so taken by Ewald's work that he threw himself into the study of the Old Testament and gave Hebrew a second try under Ewald's tutelage — his early efforts at Hebrew had been spoiled by poor and ineffective teaching.[9] His academic interests were ignited.

Ewald had more than a professorial influence on Wellhausen. The relationship was like a master to an apprentice. Under Ewald's teaching, Wellhausen studied Hebrew and the cognate Semitic languages. Smend describes Ewald's approach to philological studies as "pitiless."[10] Students who slog through Hebrew today can appreciate Wellhausen's plight, especially when one takes into account that during Wellhausen's day student-friendly approaches to the subject matter were not prevalent. Ewald's expertise in the history of Israel surpassed any of his peers during this period. Though Wellhausen eventually parted company with his teacher, his interest in reading the Bible in light of the history of Israel took form under Ewald's tutelage. In time, Wellhausen would dedicate his *Prolegomena to the History of Israel* to Ewald.

Ewald was a well-known and peculiar figure of the nineteenth century. T. K. Cheyne described him as "the great, the faulty, but the never-

---

7. Ibid.

8. Smend, "Wellhausen and His *Prolegomena*," 5; Julius Wellhausen, *Prolegomena to the History of Israel*, trans. J. S. Black and Allan Menzies (Atlanta: Scholars Press, 1994), 3.

9. Smend, *From Astruc to Zimmerli*, 92.

10. Ibid., 94.

to-be-forgotten Heinrich Ewald."[11] As a leading and productive biblical scholar of his day, he published on a wide range of Old Testament matters. Smend writes, "There was hardly a question in Old Testament scholarship to which he had not published an opinion, generally an original one, always expressed with the assurance of someone who knows the truth and defends it against the lie."[12] He wrote commentaries on biblical books and was an accomplished Semitic grammarian. Ewald published his Hebrew grammar in 1827 (he was twenty-four years old!) and worked on Arabic and Sanskrit studies. Though he wrote a biblical theology of the Old and New Testaments, Ewald was best known for his multivolume work on the history of Israel. Sharing much in common with the redemptive-historical approach of J. C. K. von Hofmann, Ewald's methodology brought the religious teachings of the Bible into close relationship with the historical development of those teachings.[13] Ewald believed in the revelatory character of the Bible.[14] He considered the location of the Bible's revelation to be found both in the religious teachings and the historical development of those teachings.

According to John Rogerson, Ewald's critical approach to the history of Israel was more traditional and theological than revisionist; it had much in common with the confessional approaches of Franz Delitzsch and, as mentioned, Hofmann.[15] Ewald stood against the Hegelian tendencies of David Friedrich Strauss and Wilhelm Vatke. De Wette was also a lifelong enemy of Ewald's. He said of de Wette, "From my youth all I have learned from him is how one should not proceed."[16] But Ewald could be equally critical of conservatives. He said of Delitzsch's commentary on Genesis, "A more superficial, careless, empty, and worthless writing on the first book of the Pentateuch than this could hardly be produced today by a

11. Quoted in John H. Hayes and Frederick Prussner, *Old Testament Theology: Its History and Development* (Atlanta: John Knox Press, 1985), 118.

12. Smend, *From Astruc to Zimmerli*, 92.

13. For more on Hofmann, see Roy A. Harrisville and Walter Sundberg, *The Bible in Modern Culture: Baruch Spinoza to Brevard Childs* (Grand Rapids: Eerdmans, 2002), 123–45. A sympathetic reading of Hofmann can be found in Robert W. Yarbrough, *The Salvation Historical Fallacy? Reassessing the History of New Testament Theology* (History of Biblical Interpretation; Leiden: Deo Publishing, 2004).

14. See Hayes and Prussner, *Old Testament Theology*, 119.

15. See John Rogerson, *Old Testament Criticism in the Nineteenth Century: England and Germany* (Minneapolis: Fortress, 1985), 101–2; for a more detailed account of Ewald's history of Israel, see Rogerson, *Old Testament Criticism*, 91–103; J. C. O'Neill, *The Bible's Authority: A Portrait Gallery of Thinkers from Lessing to Bultmann* (Edinburgh: T&T Clark, 1991), chapter 11.

16. Quoted in Rogerson, *Old Testament Criticism*, 102.

doctor of theology and university teacher in Germany."[17] Though fundamentally insecure, Ewald was his own man.[18] He fought against those who disagreed with his scholarship, his Catholicism and his politics. It was the latter that eventually led to his and Wellhausen's parting of the ways. In time, Ewald's more traditional approach to the history of Israel would also create problems for Wellhausen.[19] After Ewald's death, Wellhausen said he died "at odds with the world and in peace with God."[20]

Despite Wellhausen's tumultuous relationship with Ewald (he could not count on Ewald's help in securing a university position), Wellhausen's interest in biblical studies and the history of Israel was fixed. His particular approach to Israel's history had not yet taken shape. A fortuitous encounter, however, with Albrecht Ritschl in 1867 changed this. In a passing comment, Ritschl told the young Wellhausen of Graf's hypothesis that the law should come after the prophets in a proper history of Israel. Wellhausen recounts the event in his *Prolegomena to the History of Israel*: "I learned through Ritschl that Karl Heinrich Graf placed the law later than the prophets, and, almost without knowing the reasons for the hypothesis, I was prepared to accept it; I readily acknowledged to myself the possibility of understanding Hebrew antiquity without the book of the Torah."[21] Graf's hypothesis of a history of Israel that worked from the prophets to the law rather than the canonical presentation of the law to the prophets opened up new vistas for Wellhausen. The work for which Wellhausen is best known, his *Prolegomena*, is an extended and detailed account of Israel's history with this hypothesis framing the discussion.

Wellhausen needed a platform to pursue his academic interests. In 1870, he completed his dissertation and habilitation (a second doctoral thesis required for university teaching) at Göttingen. These two works dealt with critical problems in Chronicles and Samuel. Wellhausen was now in need of a permanent, and paying, academic post. August Dillmann of the University of Berlin (another student of Ewald's) put forward Wellhausen's name for a chair at Greifswald. He held this chair in theology from 1872 to 1882. While in this post, Wellhausen wrote some of his most substantial work on the history of Israel.

---

17. Ibid., 103.
18. See ibid.
19. Smend, *From Astruc to Zimmerli*, 92–94.
20. Ibid., 92.
21. Wellhausen, *Prolegomena*, 3–4.

In 1874, he published a study on the Pharisees and Sadducees (*The Pharisees and the Sadducees: An Investigation into a Point of Internal Jewish History*). In this work, Wellhausen argues against the dominant understanding of these two sects, namely, that they were separated by dogmatic positions. According to Wellhausen, they were separated by different outlooks on life — one being more political and the other more religious.[22] Also during this period (1872–1878), Wellhausen worked on a series of essays that eventually took published form under the title *The Composition of the Hexateuch and the Historical Books of the Old Testament*.[23]

In this work, Wellhausen reveals the fundamental separation and distinction of the Priestly source from the combined Yahwist and Elohist sources (called the Yehowist). Wellhausen called the Priestly (P) source Q, for *quattuor*, because it was the fourth major source of the documentary hypothesis: JED and P. The P source was a coherent and identifiable source reflecting the religious viewpoint of postexilic Israel. The combined J and E sources had a complex redactional history that, according to Wellhausen, cannot be neatly sorted out. Nor was Wellhausen concerned about clearly identifying J and E in their literary individuality. The combined source JE revealed the earliest expressions of Israel's preexilic religion, and this is the matter that concerned him. Here one observes a characteristic of Wellhausen's work that has contributed to its longevity. He did not want the simplicity of the whole to be lost in the minutiae of the details.[24] He was concerned about Israel's history of religion in its entirety and would not allow complicated matters whose resolution was dubious to slow him down.[25]

The Q or P source was postexilic in origin, while JE was preexilic and dated to the early monarchy (tenth or ninth century BC). The postexilic dating of the P source is a significant move on Wellhausen's part. For in this source most of the Mosaic legislation is found. If the Mosaic legislation is postexilic, then it is a later development in Israel's religion, not an ingredient aspect of their preexilic religious life. The lateness of P's Mosaic legislation is an important dimension of Wellhausen's subsequent work.

---

22. See Smend, *From Astruc to Zimmerli*, 95.
23. The Hexateuch includes the first six books of the Old Testament, Genesis to Joshua. Joshua is included in this construct because it concludes the Torah traditions of Moses and is the product of the same complex of traditions present in the Pentateuch.
24. O'Neill, *The Bible's Authority*, 200.
25. To see the details of Wellhausen's source-division, see S. R. Driver, *An Introduction to the Literature of the Old Testament* (Cleveland: Meridian, 1967), chapter 1.

In *The Composition*, Wellhausen identified the historical books of the Old Testament as a collection of older writings that had been combined with the Pentateuch and redacted (edited) along Deuteronomistic lines — that is, along lines consonant with the outlook of Deuteronomy. If Deuteronomy is removed from the picture, one has the three basic sources of the Pentateuch: J, E (combined as JE), and Q or P. The resulting picture of the Pentateuch is as follows: Deuteronomy is an independent source, while Genesis to Numbers is a redacted combination of the JE and P sources. Proper understanding of Israel's history of religion demands the literary identification and separation of these two sources.

According to Smend, "the real novelty" of the work was not so much Wellhausen's literary critical conclusions — Wellhausen refers to such attempts alone as "sport, or a game of skittles."[26] Rather, the novelty of Wellhausen's approach was his use of literary or source criticism as a means to reconstruct Israel's history.[27] Israel's literary growth represents various stages in Israel's actual historical development. This collection of essays laid the groundwork for Wellhausen's most famous work on Israel's history. The first edition was published in 1878 under the title *The History of Israel I*, while the second edition (1883), along with subsequent editions, appeared as the *Prolegomena to the History of Israel*.[28] We will examine Wellhausen's *Prolegomena* more fully in the second part of this chapter.

The publication of Wellhausen's *Prolegomena* was momentous. The ruckus caused over David Friedrich Strauss's *Life of Jesus* in 1835 compares to the stir created on account of Wellhausen's book.[29] The reaction of conservative detractors such as Franz Delitzsch and August Dillmann was sharp and polemical — Dillmann told Wellhausen by letter that his dedication of the *Prolegomena* to Heinrich Ewald could only be interpreted as a mockery.[30] This caustic response was facilitated by Wellhausen's "uninhibited tone."[31] He spoke simply, though not simplistically, and the force of his claims did not get lost in academic jargon. Smend states, "It is written in a clear and uncomplicated language, fresh and vivid, often pungent and

---

26. Quoted in Smend, *From Astruc to Zimmerli*, 95.
27. See ibid., 95 – 96.
28. *Prolegomena zur Geschichte Israels* (Berlin: Reimer).
29. Regarding Strauss, see Stephen Neill and Tom Wright, *The Interpretation of the New Testament, 1861 – 1986* (Oxford: Oxford Univ. Press, 1988), 13 – 20.
30. See Maier, *William Robertson Smith*, 178.
31. Smend, *From Astruc to Zimmerli*, 97.

funny."[32] Wellhausen was labeled a heretic. Because of his stated appreciation for Wilhelm Vatke, he was called a Hegelian — a claim that has broken down under critical scrutiny.[33] Franz Delitzsch told William Robertson Smith that Wellhausen's speculations were "merely the application of Darwinism to the sphere of theology and criticism."[34] To say the least, Wellhausen was a controversial figure whose theories created a divide both in the academy and the church.

The friendship between William Robertson Smith and Wellhausen is of special interest. Smith was a Free Church of Scotland minister and theology professor at Aberdeen. The two first met in Göttingen in 1872, and in 1878 Wellhausen asked for Smith's frank assessment of his *History*. Smith praised the work for its "largeness of view and firmness of grasp."[35] This exchange began a long-standing and extensive correspondence between the two. Wellhausen told Smith in correspondence, "There are few people in Germany who appreciate that I have actually more positive intentions than the criticism of the Pentateuch ... I am glad that it is different in Britain."[36] Smith did much to make Wellhausen's work available in English. An English edition appeared in 1885. Smith wrote the preface. Even though Smith retained an evangelical outlook, his acceptance of Wellhausen's views led to his defrocking and dismissal from his academic post. The foment around Smith's case reveals something of the ire of the times.[37]

Wellhausen's conscience began to trouble him in the midst of this turmoil. When the first edition of his *History* appeared, he was still a member of the theology faculty at Greifswald. This bothered Wellhausen because he felt misplaced and unfit to fulfill the faculty's educational purpose. He informed the minister of education in Berlin on April 5, 1882, of his resignation from the theology faculty in order to become a *Privatdozent* (an unsalaried university teacher) in Semitic Philology. He wrote:

---

32. Smend, "Wellhausen and His *Prolegomena*," 13. Smend makes mention of the mischievous "cool polemic" of the first edition that was later expunged in the second edition of 1883.

33. Ronald Clements concedes that there may be Hegelian traces in Wellhausen's work. He concludes, however, "Yet all these factors in no way amount to an overall demonstration that the rise of critical Old Testament scholarship was the product of a number of contemporary philosophical presuppositions ... The underlying conviction of their endeavors was a foundation of common truth which all could read and share" (*A Century of Old Testament Study* [Cambridge, UK: Lutterworth, 1992], 3).

34. Quoted in Smend, "Wellhausen and His *Prolegomena*," 14.

35. Quoted in Maier, *William Robertson Smith*, 178.

36. Quoted in Smend, "Wellhausen and His *Prolegomena*," 12. On the reception of Wellhausen in England, see Rogerson, *Old Testament Criticism*, chapter 20.

37. Similar stories took place in the United States in the cases of Charles Briggs in Presbyterian life and Crawford Toy in Southern Baptist controversies.

I became a theologian because the scientific treatment of the Bible interested me; only gradually did I come to understand that a professor of theology also has the practical task of preparing the students for service in the Protestant church, and that I am not adequate to this practical task, but that instead despite all caution on my own part I make hearers unfit for their office. Since then my theological professorship has been weighing heavily on my conscience.[38]

Wellhausen never had to take the role of *Privatdozent*. He was appointed *Ausserordentlicher* professor (associate professor in American university terms) in Semitic languages at the University of Halle from 1882–1885. This was a step down from his position at Greifswald, but conscience demanded this of him. He was then appointed in 1885 to a professorship in Marburg. He remained there happily until 1892. Out of respect for the Old Testament professor in Marburg, Wellhausen did not lecture on the Old Testament during this period. But after Ewald's successor in Göttingen, Paul de Lagarde, died, Wellhausen accepted this chair. Smend tells the following anecdote:

> As I was told by Walter Bauer, author of the New Testament Greek lexicon, an article in a Hannover Church newspaper is supposed to have settled the matter. According to it, if Professor Wellhausen came to Göttingen, the saying would come true: "a wild sow in the master's vineyard." At that Wellhausen immediately accepted the call.[39]

Göttingen was more pretentious than the unassuming Marburg. Wellhausen commented that in Marburg you can call your colleague a "fathead," while in Göttingen everyone carries around a secret.[40]

Wellhausen was productive during his time at Göttingen. He continued to pursue his interest in the history of Israel, which eventually led to the publication of his *Israelite and Jewish History* (1895; the final revision appeared in 1914). In this work, Wellhausen investigates a burgeoning interest in the historical foundation of Judaism for Christianity. After his work on the Arab empire in 1902, he devoted his attention to the study of the gospels.[41] Wellhausen did not trouble himself with reading the specialist literature on the subject and produced commentaries on Mark (1903),

---

38. Quoted in Smend, "Wellhausen and His *Prolegomena*," 6.
39. Ibid., 7.
40. Smend, *From Astruc to Zimmerli*, 99.
41. Ibid., 101.

Matthew (1904), and Luke (1904). In 1907, he published a commentary on John, with work on Acts and Revelation rounding out the series.[42] Wellhausen's failing health forced him into retirement at the age of sixty-nine. His final lecture was on the book of Job, which was fitting in light of his declining health. Wellhausen died on January 7, 1918.

Wellhausen's scholarly efforts were prodigious and spanned several disciplines — Old Testament history and literature, Arabic studies, and New Testament exegesis. He was wary of self-promotion and decried scholarly pretentiousness. Later in life, Wellhausen would not comment on his *Prolegomena*; he left this work to others. Wellhausen was not a theologian or a churchman, nor would he claim to be — "It strikes me as a lie," he told the ministry of education, "that I should be educating ministers of an evangelical church to which in my heart I do not belong."[43] His interests in biblical studies were focused primarily on the study of Israel's history as a natural phenomenon of the ancient past. Moreover, this history had to be reconstructed along different lines than the canonical presentation. It was this historical reconstruction that was Wellhausen's most enduring contribution to Old Testament studies.

Israel versus Judaism: Wellhausen's *Prolegomena to the History of Israel*

Wellhausen's *Prolegomena* is a landmark text in the history of Old Testament interpretation. It is often associated with the documentary hypothesis — JEDP, the four sources that compose the Pentateuch. While Wellhausen did much to clarify and solidify the source-critical approach to the Pentateuch, the documentary hypothesis is only a part of the *Prolegomena*'s grand scope. The strength of Wellhausen's work is his view of the whole, his refusal to get lost among the trees when painting his picture of the forest. Working from Karl Heinrich Graf's undeveloped hypothesis, Wellhausen reconstructed the totality of Israel's history by means of analyzing the strata of her literary sources. In fact, Wellhausen was the first to offer such a history on the basis of literary critical conclusions.[44] As Smith writes in the preface to the English edition, "The Old Testament does not furnish a history of Israel, though it supplies the materials from which such a history

---

42. For a brief rehearsal of these works, see ibid., 101 – 2.
43. Quoted in O'Neill, *The Bible's Authority*, 201.
44. See John H. Hayes, "Wellhausen as a Historian of Israel," *Semeia* 25 (1982): 55.

can be constructed."[45] Wellhausen took these materials and reconstructed Israel's history by analyzing the literary strata of the Old Testament documents. Wellhausen did not blink when criticized for reconstructing Israel's history. He retorts, "But history, it is well-known, has always to be reconstructed ... The question is whether one constructs well or ill."[46]

Wellhausen's reconstruction of Israel's history trades primarily on the following question: Where should the law of Moses be located in Israel's history? The opening paragraph states clearly, "In the following pages it is proposed to discuss the place in history of the 'law of Moses'; more precisely, the question for the history of ancient Israel, or not rather for that of Judaism, *i.e.*, of the religious communion which survived the destruction of the nation by the Assyrians and Chaldeans."[47] Much of Wellhausen's overarching purpose is stated here. Preexilic Israel is set over against exilic and postexilic Judaism as two very different expressions of Israel's religion. For Wellhausen, much of Israel's early religious life was lost when Judaism formalized the law code, which in turn displaced ancient Israel's more natural and intuitive worship. The law, therefore, as an institutional norm is set over against the preexilic freedom of Israel's ancient worship.

Wellhausen's *Prolegomena* is divided into three major sections. The first section is titled "History of the Ordinances of Worship." A main tenet of Wellhausen's history is the centralization of the cult, or Israel's formal worshiping life, to Jerusalem. This particular matter is so important to Wellhausen that he could claim toward the end of the book, "My whole position is contained in my first chapter: there I have placed in a clear light that which is of such importance for Israelite history, namely, the part taken by the prophetical party in the great metamorphosis of the worship, which by no means came about of itself."[48] Wellhausen shows how earlier literature of the Hexateuch such as JE (the combined Yahwist and Elohist sources) and the historical narratives of Judges and Samuel rarely refer to a location in Israel without mentioning an altar and a sacrifice associated with it.[49]

These high places (*bamoth*), which have their source in earlier Canaanite religion, are found throughout the whole region. Gilgal and Shiloh are well-known examples, but less notable sites such as Ophrah, Ramah, and

---

45. Wellhausen, *Prolegomena*, vii.
46. Ibid., 367.
47. Ibid., 1.
48. Ibid., 368.
49. Ibid., 17.

Nob have high places as well. According to Wellhausen, the relationship between the centralized cult in Jerusalem's temple and these various high places is complicated up until the time of Solomon. For example, Solomon sacrifices at the high place of Gibeon and is rewarded with a revelation. Later, however, no king in Israel or Judah would be left unscathed if they did not tear down these high places. What this tension reveals is a shift of attitude toward the *bamoth* taking place at some point in Israel's worshiping life. This observation is key to Wellhausen's reconstruction because it reveals a development in the history of Israel's religious viewpoint, namely, the move from a decentralized to a centralized cult.

The defining historical moment establishing the centralization of Israel's worship was the eighteenth year of Josiah's reign, 621 BC. The Josianic reforms found in 2 Kings 23 signal this move in Israel's cultic history. After "discovering" the law code in the temple, Josiah sought to bring Judah's worship in line with God's law. As a result, Josiah dealt "the first heavy blow" to the various places of worship in the regions of Judah.[50] A cursory reading of 2 Kings 23 reveals Josiah's zeal in tearing down these *bamoth.* "Yet what a vitality did the green trees upon the high mountains still continue to show!"[51] Josiah's uprooting of the high places ended up as only a pruning. After his death, they appear again in all regions of Judah, much to the prophet Jeremiah's consternation.

What is important to observe here is how Wellhausen arrives at this reconstruction. He deploys a *Tendenzkritik* of the literature as a means of deciphering its historical setting — the historical setting of its composition, not the events it narrates. The literature itself is examined to determine the *Tendenz* (tendency) or outlook of the writer. This outlook reveals the particular perspective from which the author writes and helps determine the composition's historical setting. One recalls de Wette's reading of Chronicles as an example of *Tendenzkritik.* Chronicles is of no worth as a historical document for the understanding of the monarchy's empirical history. Rather, the Chronicler's perspective reveals a postexilic setting that tells us more about postexilic Israel than preexilic Israel. For example, the Priestly influence on Chronicles reveals its later dating because such influences cannot be found in Samuel and Kings.[52] As a side note, Well-

---

50. Ibid., 27.
51. Ibid.
52. Ibid., 49.

hausen agrees and is even more vociferous in his denunciation of Chronicles' historical value.[53] *Tendenzkritik* is a major tool in the *Prolegomena* for reconstructing Israel's history by means of literary analysis.

Wellhausen analyzes Deuteronomy with this method as well. De Wette had argued earlier in the eighteenth century that Deuteronomy was not written by Moses but was probably composed during the Josianic reforms. As such, the discovery of the law code in the temple treasury (2 Kings 23:2) was not in fact a discovery but a new composition of the period. Here one observes again the combination of *Tendenzkritik* and literary analysis resulting in a different understanding of Deuteronomy's historical perspective. Deuteronomy does not reveal Israel's history in the period of Moses, as the book purports to do. Instead, Deuteronomy reveals the historical and religious outlook of the Josianic reforms. The process of reading the literature according to the purported historical setting of the text's composition is the means by which Wellhausen establishes his source-critical reconstruction of Israel's history.

The particular textual perspective or *Tendenz* Wellhausen subjects his material to is the text's view on the cult. A decentralized cult with worshiping centers in most named cities is observed in JE. With D, the move toward centralization begins, though the efforts are stalled after Josiah's death. Jeremiah's prophecy witnesses to the ongoing and deleterious effects of the high places on the far side of Josiah's death. With the Priestly writer, or P, the centralization of Israel's worship in Jerusalem is finalized. The differing perspectives on Israel's cultic life reveal the historical progression of this particular matter and require a late date for the Priestly writer. Put simply, the kind of centralized cult you find in the Priestly writer is a historical impossibility in the period before Josiah. So the Priestly material of the Pentateuch does not come from the Mosaic legislations established in Moses' time. Rather, the Priestly material is retrofitted to the time of Moses in its canonical presentation, though, in fact, it is from the postexilic period. In the rest of the *Prolegomena's* first section, Wellhausen analyses the following in the same way he engages the place of worship: sacrifice, the sacred feasts, priests and Levites, and the endowment of the clergy. These four matters reveal the same historical

---

53. For an account of the minimal scholarly shift in attitude toward Chronicles, see Hans M. Barstad, *History and the Hebrew Bible* (Forschungen zum Alten Testament; Tübingen: Mohr Siebeck, 2008), 8.

development of Israel's religion as observed in the move to centralize the cult and further support his historical reconstruction.

It is worth reviewing the major contours of Wellhausen's literary/ source-critical approach. The literary critical conclusions up to this point are as follows: JE (the combined Yahwist with Elohist sources) is the earliest layer of the Pentateuchal tradition, which at the same time witnesses to the earliest period of Israel's written history — the tenth/ninth century or the beginning of the monarchy and not really much earlier. Wellhausen viewed the material of JE as a dubious resource for the reconstruction of Israel's early history of the patriarchs and Moses.[54] (In time, others such as Hermann Gunkel, Martin Noth, and Gerhard von Rad would challenge this understanding, arguing for an earlier date of the oral traditions one finds in JE.) D, or the Deuteronomist, is the second layer of the Pentateuchal tradition. It is dated to the seventh-century Josianic reforms. P, or the Priestly writer, assumes the stability and finalization of the complex historical processes that lead to the centralization of Israel's cult. The Priestly writer's perspective demands a late, postexilic date because of its *Tendenz* (particular textual perspective). Here we see the history of Israel set along lines that are consonant with the literary analysis of the Pentateuchal sources.[55]

The second section of the *Prolegomena* is titled "The History of Tradition." In this section, Wellhausen examines Chronicles, Judges, Samuel, Kings, and the narratives of the Hexateuch. At the end of his chapter on Judges, Samuel, and Kings, Wellhausen concludes, "Thus in the question of the order of sequence of the two great bodies of laws, the history of the tradition leads us to the same conclusion as the history of the cultus."[56] In other words, the history of Israel's religious development expounded in section 1 of the *Prolegomena* is confirmed in this section as well.

As previously mentioned, the narratives of the Hexateuch do not offer much credible history. What they do offer is the ideal of Israel's ancient worship. As John Hayes describes Wellhausen's view, "The patriarchs are

---

54. Clements, *Century of Old Testament Study*, 12.

55. From a macro standpoint, Genesis to Numbers is a combination of the Yahwist, Elohist, and Priestly sources, with Deuteronomy standing as the sole presentation of the D source. For a helpful overview of the history of the documentary hypothesis, as well as identification of the sources in the Pentateuch, e.g., Yahwist in Genesis 2 – 9 and Priestly source in Genesis 1, see John Van Seters's chapter in *The Hebrew Bible Today: An Introduction to Critical Issues*, ed. Steven L. McKenzie and M. Patrick Graham (Louisville: Westminster John Knox, 1998), chapter 1.

56. Wellhausen, *Prolegomena*, 294.

primarily ideal prototypes of the true Israelite — peace-loving shepherds."[57] Wellhausen had an idealized view of Israel's preexilic worship, especially in the early days of Israel's monarchy. Worship was free, the product of an individual impulse. It was not regulated by the institutions that eventually distorted Israel's primitive worship.

At the beginning of section 2, Wellhausen has a quote from the Greek poet Hesiod: "The half is more than the whole."[58] This quote reveals Wellhausen's own disposition to the history of Israel. The preexilic period, "the half," was more valued by Wellhausen than the whole of her history, which included the postexilic developments. Smend captures Wellhausen's *Tendenz*: "It was with 'the half' that his sympathies lay, which meant that the patriarchs, kings, and prophets, acting as living people according to the impulse of their nature and their circumstances, governed neither by force or cultic institutions nor by the pattern of theological conceptuality."[59] The key figures in creating and maintaining Israel's preexilic, noninstitutional, and ethical worship were the great figures of Israel's pre-legislative life, the prophets. "The half" of Israel's history, the better part, lay with them.

The religious genius and outlook of the prophets are highly esteemed in Wellhausen's *Prolegomena*. The fossilized character of Israel's postexilic institutions are placed over against the virile character of the prophets. The distinction between prophet and institution is not one of lawless versus law-abiding figures or entities. The matter is expressed this way by Wellhausen, "Ancient Israel was certainly not without God-given bases for the ordering of human life; only they were not fixed in writing."[60] When the law became fixed in Israel's history, it lost its life-giving power.

The Ten Commandments, or Decalogue, one could argue, was a written Torah going back to Moses. But even here, Wellhausen demurs.[61] The tradition is too spotty at this point. Contradictory claims about the "ark of the covenant" housing two tablets (Exodus 20:22 – 23:19) or being written on twelve stones (Deuteronomy 31:26) render the tradition unreliable. The "ark of the covenant" as the "box of the law" is particular to later writers whose outlook is shaped by the Deuteronomistic revision. The result is

---

57. Hayes, "Wellhausen as a Historian," 48.
58. Wellhausen, *Prolegomena*, 169.
59. Smend, *From Astruc to Zimmerli*, 97.
60. Wellhausen, *Prolegomena*, 393.
61. Ibid., 392 – 93.

that the ark of the covenant was itself a special religious symbol for ancient Israel and not merely a receptacle for the law. In fact, even if the ark did contain twelve stones, nothing was written on them.[62]

Before the transition toward a written legislation in the Deuteronomic period (seventh century BC), the Torah, or law, was oral. And because it was oral and attached to the charismatic personae of the priests and prophets (figures whose identities overlapped in the preexilic period), the law was fluid and dynamic. The law flowed directly from the stream of YHWH and his servant Moses. The priests were more organized and consistent a body than the prophets, whose ministries were intermittent. But they were organically connected. "What connected them with each other was the revelation of Jehovah which went on and was kept alive in both of them."[63] Both priests and prophets were conduits for the living tradition of YHWH's instruction. But when the law moved to a written and stabilized form, prophets and priests "drew off and separated from each other," and the law lost its living dynamic.[64]

"It is a vain imagination to suppose that the prophets expounded and applied the law," states Wellhausen.[65] The prophets were not the expounders of the Mosaic law, as has been the traditional understanding of their role. The prophets are the "continuators and equals" of Moses; their words are on par with his and not subordinate to them.[66] The instruction they give to the people flows like a stream directly from YHWH himself to the prophet for the people. Because the people would not hearken to the Torah coming from the prophets, God would pour out his wrath on them. But the Torah, or instruction of the prophets, is not a written legislation exerting a pressure on the shape of their prophetic word. It is a direct word from YHWH unmediated by a sedimented Mosaic law. When the law in the Deuteronomistic age began to make its fateful move toward a written form, Israel's religion was lost and prophecy died. "With the appearance of the law came to an end the old freedom, not only in the sphere of worship, now restricted to Jerusalem, but in the sphere of religious spirit as well. There was now in existence an authority as objective as could be; and this

---

62. Ibid., 393.
63. Ibid., 397.
64. Ibid.
65. Ibid., 399.
66. Ibid.

was the death of prophecy."[67] With the death of prophecy came the death of Israel's natural, free, and impulsive worshiping life.

The religious outlook of the early monarchy (tenth and ninth century BC) was an important mingling of Yahwistic worship and political commitments to the state. Canaanite festival worship gradually became attached to the worship of YHWH as the monarchy became a fixed entity. "The relation of Jehovah to people and kingdom remained firm as a rock."[68] The theocracy of Israel was not founded on a covenantal relationship between YHWH and his people as portrayed in the canonical documents. Instead, the relationship between YHWH and Israel was a natural one whose genesis and motivation was the founding of the state and the centrality of Israel's monarchy.[69] As the age of the judges elided into a centralized monarchy, major changes in Israel's religion took place as well. The centrality of YHWH as Israel's God became organically linked with the advancement of the state.[70] Ethical monotheism and the pinnacle of Israel's preexilic religious experience were born in reaction to the comingling of YHWH worship with the gods of the surrounding nations. The indictment against the worship of foreign gods was more about the identity and advancement of the state than maintaining covenant with Israel's God.

In summary, Wellhausen's view of Israel's history can be understood as a move away from a free and uninhibited worship of the people to a stilted and lifeless religion based on written legislation (Wellhausen dates the publication of the Priestly code, P, to the year 444 BC).[71] In the preexilic period, Wellhausen describes Israel's worship as follows: "Religious worship was a natural thing in Hebrew antiquity; it was the blossom of life, the heights and depths of which it was its business to transfigure and glorify."[72] The worship (or cult) of Israel on the far side of the Josianic reforms, which are worked out more fully in the exilic and postexilic periods (sixth and fifth century BC), is portrayed as a rigid shadow of Israel's former worshiping life. For Wellhausen, when the law appeared it was the death knell of

---

67. Ibid., 402.

68. Ibid., 414.

69. Ibid., 417.

70. A henotheistic view — henotheism is the worship of a particular god, namely, the nation's, while not denying the existence of the gods of other nations — in Israel's early monarchy eventually led to decay and came under fire from the preexilic prophets.

71. Wellhausen, *Prolegomena*, 405.

72. Ibid., 77.

Israel's freedom of worship and religious spirit.[73] Not only does Wellhausen pit the genius of prophecy against the flat-footed character of institution; he also places ancient Israel in sharp contrast to postexilic Judaism.[74]

Wellhausen states the matter poignantly in the final paragraph of the *Prolegomena*. It seems a fitting way to conclude our overview of his magnum opus.

> The great pathologist of Judaism is quite right: in the Mosaic theocracy the cultus became a pedagogic instrument of discipline. It is estranged from the heart; its revival was due to old custom, it would never have blossomed again of itself. It no longer has its roots in childlike impulse, it is a dead work, in spite of all the importance attached to it, nay, just because of the anxious conscientiousness with which it was gone about. At the restoration of Judaism the old usages were patched together in a new system, which, however, only served as the form to preserve something that was nobler in its nature, but could not have been saved otherwise than in a narrow shell that stoutly resisted all foreign influences. The heathenism in Israel against which the prophets vainly protested was inwardly overcome by the law on its own ground; and the cultus, after nature had been killed in it, became the shield of supernaturalistic monotheism.[75]

Conclusion

Few of the major contours of Wellhausen's work have not come under critical scrutiny. As one would expect, his project was met with resistance from confessional Christians.[76] In Germany, confessional Old Testament scholars such as Franz Delitzsch took aim at Wellhausen's theory. In America, Princeton Theological Seminary's W. H. Green saw the significance of

73. Ibid., 402.

74. A point not lost on Wellhausen's Jewish detractors. See Yehezkel Kaufmann, *The Religion of Israel, from Its Beginnings to the Babylonian Exile*, trans. Moshe Greenberg (Chicago: Univ. of Chicago Press, 1960).

75. Wellhausen, *Prolegomena*, 425.

76. There was a strong reaction to Wellhausen's theories in Jewish scholarship as well. See especially Yaacov Shavit and Mordechai Eran, *The Hebrew Bible Reborn: From Holy Scripture to the Book of Books: A History of Biblical Culture and the Battles Over the Bible in Modern Judaism*, trans. Chaya Naor (Studia Judaica 38; Berlin: Walter de Gruyter, 2007). A critical and nuanced engagement with Wellhausen's approach can be found in Kaufmann, *Religion of Israel*. Jon Levenson points out Wellhausen's anti-Judaistic instincts and chides him for his ignorance of rabbinic sources (*The Hebrew Bible, the Old Testament, and Historical Criticism* [Louisville: Westminster John Knox, 1993], 10–21).

Wellhausen's theories and sought to refute them in writing and public lectures.[77] But there was widespread acceptance of his theories as well, even among confessionally minded Old Testament scholars. In Great Britain, the names of William Robertson Smith and Samuel R. Driver represent such reception. In the *Presbyterian Review*, Charles Augustus Briggs of Union Seminary in New York entered into a published debate with Charles Hodge and B. B. Warfield over the value of historical criticism.[78] Briggs's fate ended similarly to Smith's, with a defrocking. Needless to say, Wellhausen's work and the trajectory it set for Old Testament studies put the fox among the hens.

Wellhausen's approach to Israel's history joined together naturalist sensibilities with Romantic instincts that valued free and unfettered expression over against institutionalization. Rolf Rendtorff points out how Wellhausen is inconsistent on this account; Jeremiah is praised for his individuality as a prophet, but individualization becomes the undoing of postexilic Judaism.[79] Wellhausen's esteem for the prophets was part and parcel of this period's Old Testament scholarship, but Wellhausen overreaches when he places prophecy over against the institution.

Though Wellhausen is certainly charting his own course in his scholarly work, the influences of German idealism are hard to miss. Simply stated, idealism affirms the "ideal" or nonphysical entities of culture as the primary location of a culture's identity. Ideas, not material entities, move history forward.[80] But ideas and institutions are too organically linked to be placed in such sterile columns. As James Davison Hunter states of idealism in a different context, "Idealism leads to a naïveté about the nature of culture and its dynamics that is, in the end, fatal."[81] Subsequent work on

---

77. See Marion Ann Taylor, *The Old Testament in the Old Princeton School (1812–1929)* (San Francisco: Mellen Research Univ. Press, 1992), 229–32.

78. For a brief account of the stir created in American theological education as a result of Wellhausen's work, see Glenn T. Miller, *Piety and Profession: American Protestant Theological Education, 1870–1970* (Grand Rapids: Eerdmans, 2007), 98–112.

79. Rolf Rendtorff, *Canon and Theology: Overtures to an Old Testament Theology*, trans. Margaret Kohl (Overtures to Biblical Theology; Minneapolis: Fortress, 1993), 69.

80. For an in-depth treatment of German idealism from Herder forward, see Andrew Bowie, *Introduction to German Philosophy: From Kant to Habermas* (Cambridge, UK: Polity, 2003), 41–93.

81. James Davison Hunter, *To Change the World: The Irony, Tragedy, and Possibility of Christianity in the Late Modern World* (New York: Oxford Univ. Press, 2010), 27.

82. See especially W. McKane, "Prophet and Institution," *Zeitschrift für die Alttestamentliche Wissenschaft* (1982), 251–66; Hayes, "Wellhausen as a Historian," 55–56; and the full-length treatment of Kaufmann, *The Religion of Israel, from Its Beginnings to the Babylonian Exile*.

Wellhausen has revealed this shortcoming in his work, especially in his pitting of prophecy against institution.[82]

Still, the effects of Wellhausen's *Prolegomena* are present in today's Old Testament scholarship. In fact, much subsequent scholarship in Old Testament studies was either an expansion of his seminal ideas or a reaction against them. Though the dating of the sources is debated, the reconstruction of Israel's history on the basis of these literary sources can be viewed in standard introductions to the Old Testament to this day. Even a future detractor of Wellhausen's like William Foxwell Albright affirmed the identification of the literary sources of the Pentateuch while denying Wellhausen's dating and religious-historical conclusions. For good or for ill, Old Testament scholarship has been permanently stamped by the influence of Julius Wellhausen's literary-critical approach to reconstructing Israel's history.

FOR FURTHER READING

Clements, Ronald E. *A Century of Old Testament Study.* Cambridge, UK: Lutterworth, 1992.

Driver, S. R. *An Introduction to the Literature of the Old Testament.* Cleveland: Meridian, 1967.

Hayes, John H. "Wellhausen as a Historian of Israel." *Semeia* 25 (1982): 37 – 60.

Kaufmann, Yehezkel. *The Religion of Israel, from Its Beginnings to the Babylonian Exile.* Translated and abridged by Moshe Greenberg. Chicago: Univ. of Chicago Press, 1960.

Levenson, Jon D. *The Hebrew Bible, the Old Testament, and Historical Criticism.* Louisville: Westminster John Knox, 1993.

Maier, Bernhard. *William Robertson Smith: His Life, His Work and His Times.* Forschungen zum Alten Testament. Tübingen: Mohr Siebeck, 2009.

McKane, W. "Prophet and Institution." *Zeitschrift für die Alttestamentliche Wissenschaft* (1982), 251 – 66.

O'Neill, J. C. *The Bible's Authority: A Portrait Gallery of Thinkers from Lessing to Bultmann.* Edinburgh: T&T Clark, 1991.

Rogerson, John. *Old Testament Criticism in the Nineteenth Century: England and Germany.* Minneapolis: Fortress, 1985.

Smend, Rudolf. *From Astruc to Zimmerli: Old Testament Scholarship in Three Centuries.* Translated by M. Kohl. Tübingen: Mohr Siebeck, 2007.

———. "Julius Wellhausen and His *Prolegomena to the History of Israel.*" *Semeia* 25 (1982): 1 – 20.

Wellhausen, Julius. *Prolegomena to the History of Israel.* Translated by J. S. Black and Allan Menzies. Atlanta: Scholars Press, 1994.

HERMANN GUNKEL

(1862–1932)

The Search for Israel's Religious Experience

HERMANN GUNKEL'S SIGNIFICANCE IN TWENTIETH-CENTURY OLD TES-
tament studies cannot be overstated. Technical terms that exegesis students learn in their first or second semester of studies, such as *Sitz im
Leben* (situation in life), form criticism, and genre criticism, are bound to
his name.[1] His influence on Old Testament studies is such that one cannot engage the scholarly literature on the Pentateuch, the Psalms, and, to
a lesser extent, the Prophets without encountering his name as a major
interlocutor. Rudolf Smend highlights Gunkel's importance with the following claim: "No scholar had so deep an influence on the methods of
biblical exegesis in the mid-twentieth century as Hermann Gunkel, an
influence reaching far beyond the borders of Germany."[2] Gunkel's dominant role in twentieth-century Old Testament studies demands that attention be given to his life and work.

Gunkel's approach to Old Testament studies will be placed in the context of the history of religions school and its philosophical cousin, Romanticism. Finally, Gunkel's form-critical engagement with the Psalms will
serve to illustrate his method.

---

1. See Werner Klatt, *Hermann Gunkel: Zu seiner Theologie der Religionsgeschichte und zur Enste-
hung der formgeschichtlichen Methode* (Forschungen zur Religion und Literatur des Alten und
Neuen Testaments; Göttingen: Vandenhoeck & Ruprecht, 1969), 11.
2. Rudolf Smend, *From Astruc to Zimmerli: Old Testament Scholarship in Three Centuries*, trans.
M. Kohl (Tübingen: Mohr Siebeck, 2007), 118.

Gunkel's Life and Work

Hermann Gunkel was born on May 23, 1862, the son and grandson of Lutheran pastors. This churchly setting had a formative influence on Gunkel's choice of profession and interest in religion. Though Gunkel himself eventually parted ranks with his father's and grandfather's orthodoxy, he viewed his scholarly vocation within the university as a service to the church.[3] In this regard, Gunkel's view differed from Wellhausen's more secular outlook. Gunkel's critical work is located within the realm of religion more broadly conceived and is firmly situated within the dominant strands of the German theological tradition of the time.

Gunkel grew up in an educated home, and from a young age his intellectual interests gravitated toward religion, history, and literature.[4] As we will see, the interface of these three disciplines formed the framework for Gunkel's lifework. When he entered the University of Göttingen in March 1881, Gunkel sat under the best and brightest in the German liberal theological tradition. As with most who studied under Albrecht Ritschl, Gunkel was smitten with his professor and attended Ritschl's lectures on Romans, New Testament theology, and dogmatics.[5] Ritschl's theology brought together a historicist approach to Christianity with an internalized individual experience. Both historicism and individual experience will become important categories in Gunkel's Old Testament interpretation.

In fact, during Gunkel's student days and into the 1890s, Ritschl's "school" dominated the theological climate of the German universities and churches.[6] Though the Ritschlian school defies simple definition, Bruce McCormack understands the central tenet of Ritschl's approach as "historical enquiry."[7] God's revelation of himself in the *historical* person of Jesus Christ provides an objective basis for doing theology. As such, Ritschl's theological approach was thoroughly modern, seeking to ground theology in historical facts while opposing the Romantic turn to the subjective, as seen in Schleiermacher's theology and Hegel's speculative idealism. Ritschl's theology rejected metaphysical abstraction and sought to ground theology in historical fact. McCormack shows that Ritschl's stu-

---

3. See Smend, *From Astruc to Zimmerli*, 118.
4. Ibid.; see also, Klatt, *Hermann Gunkel*, 17.
5. Smend, *From Astruc to Zimmerli*, 120.
6. See Bruce L. McCormack, *Karl Barth's Critically Realistic Dialectical Theology: Its Genesis and Development 1909–1936* (Oxford: Oxford Univ. Press, 1995), 38.
7. Ibid., 39.

dent Wilhelm Hermann, who in turn distances himself from Ritschl's historical positivism, appreciated very much his teacher's "insistence upon the independence of religion from the natural sciences and philosophy."[8] This particular aspect of Ritschl's program had an enduring element to it and can even be seen, though substantially reworked according to a different theological account, in the work of Karl Barth. On the other hand, both the grounding of Christian theology in historical criticism and the unearthing of the real, *historical* Jesus unraveled with the developing history of religions school.[9] A younger generation of "Ritschlian" scholars located in the history of religions was now on the scene. Their influence on young Gunkel was significant.

In the middle of his Göttingen studies, Gunkel spent three semesters at the University of Gießen. While there, Gunkel studied under Adolf von Harnack and Bernard Stade. The former proved to be one of the most influential figures in Gunkel's developing thought, while the latter's vacated teaching chair would, in due course, be filled by Gunkel.[10] With Stade, Gunkel was brought face-to-face again with the literary critical trajectory set by Julius Wellhausen, a tradition from which Gunkel's own work would free itself as he charted a new course. With Harnack, Gunkel's understanding of historical progression and the value of historical epochs in their own right would be reinforced (our attention will turn to this in the next section). Gunkel believed Harnack played a leading role in his development as a scholar. Gunkel dedicated his 1910 Genesis commentary to "[Adolf von Harnack] the man among all my theological teachers from whom, next to my father, I have learned most and whose cordial goodwill accompanied my decades of study."[11] Harnack was a teacher, colleague, and friend to Gunkel for most of his academic life.

After returning to Göttingen, Gunkel came under the influence of the younger contingent of the religious-historical "Ritschlian" school mentioned earlier. Gunkel referred to this school as a "little faculty" (*kleine Fakultät*), a "school" that was really without teachers and, more importantly,

---

8. Ibid., 50.

9. Ibid., 39–40. For a fuller account and critique of Ritschl's theology, especially as it pertains to his understanding of justification and the kingdom of God, see Karl Barth, *Protestant Theology in the Nineteenth Century*, trans. B. Cozens and J. Bowden (Grand Rapids: Eerdmans, 2002), 640–47; Brevard S. Childs, *Biblical Theology of the Old and New Testaments: Theological Reflection on the Christian Bible* (Minneapolis: Fortress, 1992), 626–27, 630.

10. Smend, *From Astruc to Zimmerli*, 120.

11. Hermann Gunkel, *Genesis*, trans. M. E. Biddle (Macon: Mercer Univ. Press, 1997), v.

without students.[12] It was, rather, a circle of younger teachers, a group of interrelated friends bound by an interest in religious-historical study of the Bible.[13] Members of this "young faculty" were indeed a notable group whose collective mark would be indelible on the future of biblical studies into the twentieth century. Notables such as William Wrede, Wilhelm Bousset, Ernst Troeltsch (who came later), and Hermann Gunkel himself made up the roster. The uncontested leader of this circle was the church historian Albert Eichhorn.

If not for Hugo Gressmann's work, *Albert Eichhorn and the Religious-Historical School* (1914), Eichhorn's role as leader within the developing history of religions school may have been lost.[14] His literary corpus amounts to two articles during the height of this developing school and a later article written on the Eucharist in the New Testament. This literary output is meager when compared to Wrede, Bousset, Troeltsch, and Gunkel. Its scarcity is due in part to Eichhorn's failing health. Understandably, Gressmann describes Eichhorn's role as that of a "midwife" (*Hebammendienste*) that served the birthing of the school more than establishing his name as the major contributor to it.[15] After reading Gressmann's book, Walter Baumgartner (a later student of Gunkel) was astonished to discover in Eichhorn all he had come to associate with Gunkel.[16] In retrospect, one observes Eichhorn's major influence on Gunkel's developing religious-historical sensibility.[17]

Gunkel completed his Göttingen doctoral dissertation in 1888 under the title *The Influence of the Holy Spirit on the Apostle Paul: A Biblical Theological Study*.[18] Gunkel's subtitle, according to Rudolf Smend, did not measure up to the content of the book for several reasons. First, Gunkel did not limit himself to the canonical documents. Second, Gunkel's work was not a theological study of the Spirit in relation to Paul. Gunkel had his sights on the overly idealized understanding of Spirit inherited from

---

12. Klatt, *Hermann Gunkel*, 20.
13. Ibid., 20 – 21.
14. English translation of *Albert Eichhorn und die religionsgeschichtliche Schule*. See especially Klatt, *Hermann Gunkel*, 21 – 24.
15. Klatt, *Hermann Gunkel*, 22.
16. Ibid.
17. For more information on Eichhorn, see "Eichhorn," in *Dictionary of Biblical Interpretation*, ed. John H. Hayes (Nashville: Abingdon, 1999), 1:324 – 25.
18. Hermann Gunkel, *The Influence of the Holy Spirit: The Popular View of the Apostolic Age and the Teaching of the Apostle Paul*, trans. R. A. Harrisville and P. A. Quanbeck II (Philadelphia: Fortress, 1979).

the Hegelian tradition. Smend states, "Above all he relativized the theological doctrine of the Spirit by understanding it as the interpretation of psychological processes, pneumatic experiences, which interested him as a historian of religion more than the 'concepts of biblical theology' ..."[19] Gunkel was not interested in the supernatural side of Pauline thought, that is, that God communicates his presence to his people by the Holy Spirit. His interest lay with the *perceived* influence of the Spirit in the history of religious experience.

As one can tell from the subject matter of Gunkel's dissertation, he began his scholarly work in the New Testament. It seemed to young Gunkel that the New Testament was the proper location to wage a debate with Ritschl over the nature of historical inquiry.[20] All Ritschlians were concerned with historical investigation. The newer generation of Ritschlians, however, found the dogmatic assumptions of Ritschl untenable and ultimately obfuscating of historical inquiry. McCormack labels the older Ritschlians as "ecclesially oriented," while the newer generation was "scientifically oriented."[21] This New Testament emphasis can also be seen in the other members of the "little faculty" — Wrede, Troeltsch, Bousset, and even Eichhorn. Gunkel began teaching at Göttingen for a semester. He moved to Halle to teach New Testament but was opposed by the faculty there. This "certain stroke of fate" resulted in Gunkel's forced exile to Old Testament.

Hereafter, Gunkel's primary scholarly pursuits were in Old Testament, even though he maintained an interest in the New Testament's place in the history of religions.[22] Gunkel lectured in Halle until 1895, when he was appointed associate professor at Berlin. Just before his move to Berlin, Gunkel completed in 1894 his first major Old Testament work, *Creation and Chaos in the Primeval Era and the Eschaton*.[23] In this work, Gunkel places Israel's creation myths, or *sagas*, as Gunkel would have it, in the context of their religious and historical milieu in the ancient Near East. The author of Genesis 1 (P for Gunkel) is indebted to old traditions that were adopted from Israel's ancestral neighbors.[24] Instead of searching for

---

19. Smend, *From Astruc to Zimmerli*, 121–22.
20. Klatt, *Hermann Gunkel*, 29.
21. McCormack, *Barth's Critically Realistic Dialectical Theology*, 41.
22. Smend, *From Astruc to Zimmerli*, 122–23.
23. *Schöpfung und Chaos in Urzeit und Endzeit* (Göttingen: Vandenhoeck & Ruprecht, 1895).
24. See Douglas A. Knight, *Rediscovering the Traditions of Israel*, 3rd ed. (Studies in Biblical Literature; Atlanta: Society of Biblical Literature, 2006), 60.

literary sources as Wellhausen did, Gunkel's interest lay with the traditions of Israel, their preliterary form, their location in ancient Near Eastern religion, and the way Israel's religious tradition incorporated and actualized these materials with their own particular stamp. Gunkel's approach placed a heavy emphasis on the oral nature of Israel's traditions. He stressed that these very old myths in Israel's religious life originated as an oral rather than a written tradition. The seed for Gunkel's form-critical approach is sown in this book.

Gunkel was an inspiring teacher. Karl Barth recounts sitting under Gunkel and having the spirit of the Old Testament laid bare before him. In these lectures, Barth first came to believe that the Old Testament was a possibility for his own advanced study.[25] Smend tells of the higher-than-average attendance at Gunkel's lectures and the influence he had on a whole range of students.[26] Gunkel's strengths as a scholar and teacher were confirmed with his appointment to a chair at Gießen in 1907. This appointment came rather late in Gunkel's academic and publishing career, a fact revealing his underappreciated status by fellow biblical scholars.[27] Gunkel remained in this chair until failing health forced him into retirement in 1927. He had to relinquish much of his writing plans and focused his attention on his *Introduction to the Psalms*. The work became too much for Gunkel, and he entrusted the completion of his Psalms work to his student Joachim Begrich during Christmas 1931. Gunkel died on March 11, 1932. His *Introduction to the Psalms* appeared the following year.

Gunkel's literary output included an exposition of Genesis. The English translation is titled *The Stories of Genesis* (1901). This work is considered a classic to this day.[28] Even in Gunkel's day, the book went through five revisions, resulting in the massive 1910 *Genesis* commentary. He produced a work on the Prophets in 1917, was a coeditor and major contributor to *Religion in History and the Present*, the most important German encyclopedia on the subject, and devoted himself to the Psalms for the majority of his time in Gießen.[29] Gunkel's great strength was his ability to take the forms

---

25. See Eberhard Busch, *Karl Barth: His Life from Letters and Autobiographical Texts*, trans. John Bowden (Grand Rapids: Eerdmans, 1975), 39.

26. Smend, *From Astruc to Zimmerli*, 124.

27. See Ronald E. Clements, *A Century of Old Testament Study* (Cambridge, UK: Lutterworth, 1992), 14.

28. See Smend, *From Astruc to Zimmerli*, 125.

29. *Die Religion in Geschichte und Gegenwart* (Tübingen: Mohr Siebeck, 1913).

and structures of the Bible and make them come alive within the contours of life in Israel's own religious history. From the perspective of the canonical function of Scripture within the church, his greatest strength was also his Achilles' heel.

Romanticism and Religious History

Gunkel's literary and religious instincts are located on the trajectory set by the German Romantics. It is important to see how the history of religions school takes its impetus and scholarly sensibility from this particular philosophical trajectory. Gunkel's work appears over a hundred years after the *Sturm und Drang* (storm and stress) decade of the 1770s. This movement in German culture stood in direct opposition to the overly rationalistic outlook of the Enlightenment and brought with it, in Charles Taylor's terms, "a revolution in German literature and criticism, which was decisive for the future of German culture."[30] The key figure in this Romantic reaction in German culture was a figure we met with W. M. L. de Wette, namely, Johann Gottfried Herder. The expressivist anthropology of Herder, or the belief that the primary function of human beings is to express themselves, had a shaping influence on the next century of German thought, as seen, for example, in the literary work of Johann Wolfgang Goethe. Gunkel is a grandchild, if you will, of the German Romantics. He is not interested in a purely rationalistic approach to biblical studies in which the interpreter detaches himself or herself from the subject studied. Gunkel's interest is that of religion and the historical progression of religious thought in various epochs of civilization. "Would to God," Gunkel wrote in the *Christliche Welt* in 1900, "I had a voice that could pierce the heart and conscience of theological researchers. I should cry out day and night nothing but this message: Never forget your sacred duty to your people! Write for the educated! Speak not so much of literary criticism, text criticism, archaeology, and all the other scholarly things, but speak of *religion*! Think of the main issue! Our people thirst for your words on *religion* and its *history*."[31] *Religion* and *history* especially as seen in Israel's literary traditions are the focal points of Gunkel's approach. Before turning to the specifics of Gunkel's

---

30. Charles Taylor, *Hegel* (Cambridge: Cambridge Univ. Press, 1975), 13.

31. Quoted in J. C. O'Neill, *The Bible's Authority: A Portrait Gallery of Thinkers from Lessing to Bultmann* (Edinburgh: T&T Clark, 1991), 230.

form-critical method, a quick overview of Romanticism and the history of religions school is necessary.

In his lucid and insightful book *The Roots of Romanticism*, Isaiah Berlin states that there are three propositions on which Western thought rests. The Enlightenment, or the turn to the self's own autonomous rationality and self-sufficiency, is specifically related to these three. I mention these three because they are the philosophical impulses against which Romanticism reacted.

1. All genuine questions can be answered. If a question cannot be answered, it is not a question. Even if we cannot answer it now due to our weakness or stupidity, someone in due course will be able to. If something is not knowable, then something is fundamentally wrong with the question.

2. All answers to real questions are knowable, and this knowledge can be transferred to others. There are means that we have within our reach to answer all real questions.

3. All answers must be compatible with one another, because if they are not compatible, then there would be chaos. One proposition cannot contradict another proposition. If the sun is the center of the universe, then the moon cannot be. One comes to these conclusions by reason. In the maths, one arrives at these propositions deductively as practitioners move from general theories and then move to address the particularity of problems by means of these general theories. In science and nature, conclusions are arrived at inductively. Preconceived notions are set aside, and one observes the outside world for what it is. From this neutral observation, conclusions are drawn.[32]

According to Berlin, Enlightenment thinkers believed that even though we may live in a world that looks like a jigsaw puzzle, it can in fact be put together into a meaningful whole, even if only by God himself. The belief was that a scientific approach could be taken to morality or ethics, just as Isaac Newton observed the world around him with scientific skills of observation and analysis. These too can be inductively arrived at with the same scientific approach. The confidence found in math and science could be moved into the more complex fields of aesthetics, ethics, and politics.

32. See Isaiah Berlin, *The Roots of Romanticism* (Princeton, N.J.: Princeton Univ. Press, 2001), 21 – 23.

Though the Enlightenment is not a monolithic entity, Berlin posits that what is common to all Enlightenment thinkers is the belief that virtue is found in knowledge.[33] The Romantic movement reacted strongly against many of these foundations of Enlightenment thought.

Romanticism had its roots in Germany's pietistic tradition, while at the same time it shared the Enlightenment's skepticism regarding the theological foundation of pietism. Romanticism emphasized the experiential and the expressive over against the detachment of Enlightenment rationalism, and it also denied biblical revelation's governing role in our approach to the expressive and the experiential. Berlin describes the movement:

> As for its [Romanticism's] causes, I can only repeat my previous suggestion, namely, that it was largely due both to the intense spirituality of the pietism from which these people spring, and to the ravages of science, which undermined their pietistic faith and, while leaving them with the temperament of pietists, had removed the religious certainties of that movement.[34]

This is an extremely important quote because it begins to get at the heart of the shift taking place in Old Testament studies during this time. The Romantic move away from detached observation, obscure rationalism, and pure induction rooted in the scientific method is a move toward passion. Passion cannot be quantified or dissected. Passion has to do with feeling, being, and expression.

Since the theological foundation of Romanticism's pietistic parents had been called into question, or better, God's revelatory character had been set aside, now the source of this feeling, being, and expression was to be found in humanity itself. Here theology becomes religion, and the quest for the divine becomes one with the quest for that which is authentically human, i.e., expressivist anthropology. The Romantics have to look for "religion" in something other than revelation; it will now be found in the humanities in general or in the course of traceable human history with all its *Sturm und Drang* (storm and stress). The scientific optimism of the Enlightenment is replaced with the tragic, as conflict and tragedy become the fabric of the universe. Puccini's opera *La bohème*, with all of its struggling artists and unrequited love, illustrates the scene well.

The Enlightenment's cold and calculating rationality had as its

---

33. Ibid., 25.
34. Ibid., 55.

countervailing voice the Romantic understanding of human nature as primarily expressive in orientation. Charles Taylor observes, "The central notion is that human activity and human life are seen as expressions."[35] Art illustrates the point. In the period of the Enlightenment, a piece of art was measured by its adherence to assumed governing principles of form, symmetry, composition, and beauty. The expressive impulse of the Romantics, however, valued a piece of art for the expression of the artist, despite its conforming to particular governing rules of aesthetics. The expression of the individual via the medium of art is more important that the finished product's conformity to a particular standard.

Judging art by a set standard becomes especially difficult when the history of art is taken into account. To judge the ancient Greek's artwork by modern standards is to run roughshod over the particularity of the Greeks in their time and place. Berlin's quote explains the matter:

> Unless you understand what the Greeks were, what they wanted, how they lived, unless ... by an act of enormous difficulty, with the greatest possible effort of the imagination, you enter into the feelings of these exceedingly strange peoples, remote from you in time and place, unless you try by some act of imagination to reconstruct within yourself the form of life which these people led, what their laws were, what their ethical principles were, what their streets looked like, what their various values were, unless you try in other words to live yourself into their form of life ... your chances of truly understanding their art and truly understanding their various writings and really knowing what Plato meant and really knowing who Socrates was are small.[36]

And now we come closer to the particular influence Romantic thought had on the religious-historical school's approach to biblical studies. The Old Testament becomes a source for the reconstruction of the ancient world of the Hebrews and, more importantly, a source for understanding ancient Israel's religion as found in their own religious expression.

As we saw with de Wette, the German philosopher Johann Herder is a major voice for the Romantic shift that was taking place.[37] The search for

---

35. Taylor, *Hegel*, 14.

36. Berlin, *Roots of Romanticism*, 62.

37. Hermann Gunkel clearly states Herder's influence on his thought ("Why Engage the Old Testament?" in *Water for a Thirsty Land: Israelite Literature and Religion*, ed. K. C. Hanson [Minneapolis: Fortress, 2001], 4). On Herder's influence on de Wette's Psalms work, which in turn influenced Gunkel, see Klatt, *Hermann Gunkel*, 230–35.

that which is authentically human is the search for that which is particular to oneself and to particular cultures as well. Taylor describes Herder's thought as the valuing of personal ownership of our own human essence. The converse is the recognition that someone else's identity or essence is *not* my own. Others — and, more importantly for our purposes, other cultures — have a way of being human unlike our own. To miss this dynamic is to run the risk of "distortion and self-mutilation."[38] In other words, the French are not the Germans. The Russians are not Africans. Moreover, *ancient Israel is neither modernity nor Christianity; it is ancient Israel.*

Listen to Herder's description of this hermeneutical process as it relates to Old Testament studies:

> Become with shepherds a shepherd, with a people of the sod a man of the land, with the ancients of the Orient an Easterner, if you wish to relish these writings in the atmosphere of their origin; and be on guard especially against abstractions of dull, new academic prisons, and even more against all so-called artistry which our social circles force and press on those sacred archetypes of the most ancient days.[39]

The concern for the historical, which religious history affirms, is not a purely descriptive task. It is a task located in our ability as humans to empathize with other peoples and enter into their world. In this approach to ancient Israel, the search for the historical is the search for the human religious expression in a culture different from ours and, more to the point, different from Christianity.[40]

The religious-historical school emphasizes natural religion over against revelatory religion.[41] Gunkel states the matter starkly: "The Old Testament reveals its true greatness only when we have made up our minds to surrender unreservedly the ancient doctrine of inspiration. We have brought it down from heaven to earth, and now it rises majestically before our eyes from earth to heaven."[42] The majesty of the Old Testament for Gunkel is located in the religious expression and feeling of the people at that time

---

38. Taylor, *Hegel*, 15.

39. Quoted in Hans Frei, *The Eclipse of Biblical Narrative: A Study in Eighteenth and Nineteenth Century Hermeneutics* (New Haven, Conn.: Yale Univ. Press, 1974), 185.

40. Though Gunkel does affirm that the New Testament's religious foundation is the Old Testament, he also conceives of the Old Testament's religious history as unique in its own right, apart from Christianity's claims about Jesus ("Why Engage the Old Testament?" 13–15).

41. See Hans-Joachim Kraus, *Geschichte der historisch-kritischen Erforschung des Alten Testaments*, 3rd ed. (Neukirchen-Vluyn: Neukirchener Verlag, 1982), 327.

42. Gunkel, "Why Engage the Old Testament?" 26.

Crudely put, this is a "bottom up" approach to the subject matter of the Old Testament. The notion that the Scriptures of Israel have a canonical life of their own beyond their original setting as a continuing normative witness to God's self-disclosure is an erroneous superstition of the past needing to be displaced.

As such, this school did not rest their own Christian religion on the historical character of the Old or New Testaments or on the truth claims of these documents. Rather, religion is an inner dynamic not beholden to the normativity of the biblical documents. As a result of this religious instinct, there was great freedom in the reading of the biblical documents in their particular historical setting. Not much was at stake regarding the religious-historical conclusions of the study of ancient Israel or Jesus and the early church. Gunkel states, "We are not entitled to select from the course of history some isolated facts or some entire periods and declare that these and these alone are of God and supernatural."[43] Again, modernity is not antiquity, and the biblical documents born out of the ancient Near East or the Hellenistic world have no canonical status for those reading them. They are the record of Israel's ancient religious impulses and practices and need to be read along these lines.

Gunkel's critical approach to the Old Testament should be located within this broader religious-historical trajectory, though he definitely places his own stamp on the discipline. For Gunkel, ancient Israel was a part of the larger religious milieu of ancient Mesopotamia and Egypt. This religious-comparative approach is seen in his work on Genesis. Gunkel thought Wellhausen's source-critical approach was too limiting. He wanted to press beyond Wellhausen's identification of literary sources to the religious setting of ancient Israel in the context of her ancient Near Eastern neighbors and the cosmological/cosmogonical traditions they held in common.[44] The early work of Gunkel focused on the comparative method of analyzing Israel's religious traditions, especially in their oral phase and in light of Israel's ancient Near Eastern context. Gunkel's later work on Genesis and Psalms tended to move away from the comparative method alone, with more detailed attention given to the nature of Israel's literary deposits.[45] In this later move, now identified as the form-critical

---

43. Quoted in "Religionsgeschichtliche Schule," in *Dictionary of Biblical Interpretation*, 1:386.

44. See Hermann Gunkel, *Creation and Chaos in the Primeval Era and the Eschaton*, trans. K. William Whitney Jr. (Grand Rapids: Eerdmans, 2006), 5 – 6.

45. The comparative method will be discussed more fully in the chapter on William Foxwell Albright.

approach, Gunkel's aesthetic and literary appreciation allowed him to locate Israel's religion in the various literary forms and genres present in the biblical documents, especially the Psalms. Our attention turns now to an examination of Gunkel's form-critical approach.

Gunkel's Form Criticism and the Psalms

Consider this quote from Gunkel's *Introduction to Psalms*:

> So many recent Old Testament researchers of aesthetic research harbor a mistrust that is all too frequently materially unfounded. They are accustomed to maintaining from the outset that every aesthetic observation or argumentation is subjective. They shove to the side as "unscientific," or they rather inartistically contrast the bare "word" to the content as something of lesser value.[46]

These words from Gunkel help orient us to his particular approach to this corpus of Israel's religious history. The very nature of the psalms and their initial setting in Israel's religious life demands a more subjective approach to the material. Cool detachment will not suffice because the material itself demands sensitivity to a literature quite different from modern modes of expression. The key, therefore, is to understand the particular forms or literary types as an entry point for our understanding of this collection and the "real life" from which it arose.

The psalms themselves, for Gunkel, create a number of difficulties that need to be overcome.[47] The manner of speech found in Hebrew poetry is foreign to us. Here Gunkel explains the terse nature of Hebrew poetry, which often enjambs short sentences, or cola, onto each other with no linguistic connections. "The LORD is my shepherd. I shall not want." Gunkel compares the psalms to chimes (*Glockenspiel*) whose tones reverberate "powerfully and magnificently," but it demands a certain amount of knowledge from the reader to put the pieces together (a knowledge Gunkel hopes to provide).[48]

The psalms by their very nature have an indeterminate way of expression. In other words, the psalmist never quite fills in the blanks for the

---

46. Hermann Gunkel, *Introduction to Psalms: The Genres of the Religious Lyric of Israel*, trans. J. D. Nogalski (Macon, Ga.: Mercer Univ. Press, 1998), 16.
47. Ibid., 1 – 3.
48. Ibid., 1.

reader regarding the particularity of the events out of which the psalm arose. For example, complaint psalms rarely mention the specifics of their circumstances that led to the complaint. Allusions and imagery are used to heighten the nature of the language and the poetic sense of the psalms, but modern readers are often left scratching their heads as they try to make sense of the allusion's point or referent, e.g., "Strong bulls of Bashan encircle me" (Psalm 22:12). Moreover, the psalms are filled with "passion."[49] The impulse to hyperbole from the psalmist can be offensive to modern ears. Gunkel states that modern biblical scholars are praised for their "sobriety" as interpreters, but what one finds in the psalms is the hot blood of Hebrew poets.[50]

The list of difficulties continues for Gunkel. The use of Hebrew tense forms makes it difficult to track the perspective of the author. Is the author speaking from the present or rehearsing past events? Because the psalms tend to be short, making sense of them is a challenge, whereas if the psalms were longer, there might be opportunity to clarify ambiguities. Also, the poems lack credible traditions; the psalms' titles cannot be trusted; and the editors of the material did a very poor job keeping track of the psalms' origin. In other words, it takes creative and diligent work to locate the psalms in their original setting because the Hebrew text of the psalms is littered with problems. Finally, there seems to be no rationale for the internal ordering of the psalms.[51] Gunkel quotes Goethe to illustrate his point, "It has nothing behind it. It stands alone, and must tell you everything."[52] But these problems have to be overcome for Gunkel because the "unbreakable principle of scholarship" is that "nothing can be understood outside of its context."[53] Because of this "unbreakable principle," Gunkel conceives of the primary task of Psalms studies as "rediscover[ing] the relationships between individual songs."[54] The great gap in understanding the relationship between the psalms is the window of opportunity in Gunkel's program for unlocking their mystery.

---

49. Ibid.

50. Ibid., 2.

51. This particular "difficulty" rehearsed from Gunkel has been thoroughly challenged in recent Psalms' scholarship. See, for example, J. Clinton McCann Jr., *A Theological Introduction to the Book of Psalms: The Psalms as Torah* (Nashville: Abingdon, 1993); Brevard S. Childs, *Introduction to the Old Testament as Scripture* (Philadelphia: Fortress, 1979), 504–25.

52. Gunkel, *Psalms*, 3.

53. Ibid.

54. Ibid.

Gunkel's project attempts to relate the individual songs to one another by analyzing their various forms.[55] Because religious-historical context is so decisive in Gunkel's approach, it is "irrelevant" whether the songs are to be found inside or outside the canon, inside or outside Israel.[56] One must look to the narrative and prophetic books of the Old Testament, as well as to the Apocrypha, New Testament, and the cultic expressions found in the Babylonian and Assyrian literature. In his Psalms work, Gunkel is more interested in the literary aspect of the material than he was in his earlier *Creation and Chaos*. Still, one observes his religious-historical instincts at work. Israel's poetic sensibility is located within a larger cross-current of ancient Near Eastern expression. All of these various poetic expressions provide the researcher with the materials needed to analyze and codify the various forms of cultic poetry.

Again, Gunkel is seeking "to bring light and order" to this disparate and diverse collection of material now known as the Psalter.[57] The following is a key methodological statement from Gunkel: "Accordingly, *genre research* in the Psalms is nonnegotiable, not something one can execute or ignore according to preferences. Rather, it is *the foundational work* without which there can be no certainty in the remainder. It is the firm ground from which everything else must stand."[58] Without genre identification, for Gunkel, the student of the psalms is left without a compass or ballast on very high seas. Everything rises or falls on the identification of genres (*Gattungen*) or forms.

In spite of Gunkel's clarion call for the centrality of biblical forms, the student is still left with the methodological question, "How does one identify a genre?" For Gunkel, the attempt at genre identification cannot be abstract or arbitrary; it must flow from "the character of the material itself."[59] And here we see Gunkel's Romantic sense in full gear. One must

---

55. *Form* and *Gattung* (genre) are often used interchangeably in form-critical studies. The slight difference between the terms is as follows: *Form* has to do with identifiable "formal" aspects of a literary type. For example, an acceptance speech at the Oscars tends to begin with thanking the Academy for presenting the recipient with this honor. This is the formal aspect of the Oscar speech that is identifiable and transferable between various speeches. The *Gattung* is the actual literary type that has these formal elements within it, and thus identifies the speech as an "Oscar acceptance speech." See John Barton, *Reading the Old Testament: Method in Biblical Study*, rev. ed. (Louisville: Westminster John Knox, 1996), 250–51.

56. Gunkel, *Psalms*, 3.

57. Ibid., 5.

58. Ibid.

59. Ibid., 7.

recognize the material of the psalms as having been born out of *real life*. The literary deposits serve as windows onto the real life situation out of which the psalms arose. "In real life women sing the victory song to those returning, triumphant armies. In real life some of the professional mourners strike up the moving dirge over the one who has passed away."[60] Gunkel had imbibed Herder's invitation for scholars of the Old Testament to enter the world of the shepherd and become a shepherd, to imagine the historical particularity of a people group unlike your own without imposing your own categories and forms on them. The search for the psalm's original, "real life" setting is the search for the psalm's *Sitz im Leben* (situation in life). Though historical context is an aspect of *Sitz im Leben*, care must be taken not to reduce the term to historical context alone. The *Sitz im Leben* has to do with the sociological, cultural, and religious setting that made possible the particular literary form one encounters in the Bible.

Moreover, for Gunkel, the primary original setting of the various forms or genres now found in the literary deposit of the Psalter is Israel's cult, or worshiping life.[61] It is in the worshiping rites of Israel's religious-historical situation where light is going to be shed on the various categories of the psalms. The psalms themselves witness to a compositional growth by gradual accretion — in the combining of literary forms into one psalm, for example. Therefore, one must press behind some of the more complex psalms that mix various genres in order to arrive at "the oldest worship service."[62] Because the oldest genres were "pure and simple" without the mixture of genres, the earlier layers of Israel's traditions are prized over later ones.[63]

By way of example, Psalm 40 exhibits all the character traits of what Gunkel refers to as a "thanksgiving psalm."

> I waited patiently for the LORD;
>> he turned to me and heard my cry.
> He lifted me out of the slimy pit,
>> out of the mud and mire;
> he set my feet on a rock
>> and gave me a firm place to stand.
>
> PSALM 40:1 – 2

---

60. Ibid.
61. Ibid.
62. Ibid., 8.
63. Ibid., 19.

The psalmist is standing outside the deep end of the pool, thanking God for delivering him from the particular trouble he was facing. A move is made in verse 11, however, that sounds more like a lament psalm than a thanksgiving psalm. Now the form-critic has a problem because one psalm has a mixture of genres. Here Gunkel, and the form-critical trajectory set by him, would have to divide the psalm in two because two original life settings are operative in one psalm. The latter part is an obvious accretion, or later addition (genre mixing), and must be dealt with in a different context because the original form of the genres were pure, simple, and unmixed.[64] Again, earlier layers of the tradition are valued over later accretions. To put it another way, the psalms as we have them now in their canonical shaping are an obstacle to identifying the purity and simplicity of Israel's original worship setting.

Gunkel was assured that religion in the ancient time of the Hebrews was at its zenith in the worship service. The hostility one might find toward the cult in the Latter Prophets — one thinks of Isaiah 58's invective against cultic fasting and Sabbath keeping — has to represent a later stage in Israel's religious development.[65] Its earliest stages, however, valued the worship service as the pinnacle of religious experience. Even the highly individual complaint psalms within the Psalter had their original forms within the sanctuary. In other words, the psalms of the pious individual in the Psalter were borrowing an older form already active and preserved within Israel's cult. Gunkel states, "Accordingly, we can accept that, even in Israel, *the pious individual did not sing the first psalms* in order to pour out his most personal thoughts before God. Rather, *the priests composed* these psalms and preserved them at the sanctuary in order to use them at appropriate occasions."[66] Gunkel lays out a process for identifying psalms and locating them in their original life setting.

The Psalms researcher must first identify the particular genre of the psalm. Gunkel warns that such a task must follow strict guidelines. He believes that if these "three demands" are followed, then subjectivity will be kept at bay.

1. Look for a grouping together of various psalms that are related to a

---

64. This approach to Psalm 40 can be observed in Kraus's otherwise fine commentary on Psalms (*Psalms 1–59: A Continental Commentary* [Minneapolis: Fortress, 1987]).

65. Wellhausen's genetic history of Israel's religion overlaps with Gunkel at this point.

66. Gunkel, *Psalms*, 13.

"specific *occasion(s) in the worship service.*" The psalms themselves provide the clues into the particular worship setting. For example, one looks for textual clues related to preparation for battle or holy dance or festival processions within the psalm itself as a window onto the particular life setting.

2. The songs that belong to a particular form should share "a common *treasury of thoughts and moods.*"

3. A certain aesthetic consideration is "absolutely necessary" — that of recognizing common language shared between psalms that is related to the particularity of that form.[67] In Gunkel's terms, psalms related to each other by form or genre classification share a "preferred vocabulary" common to that particular form. In other words, hymns have a linguistically shared "hymnic" language; royal psalms do so as well. Psalms readers need to be aware of this aesthetic sensibility to make sense of the psalms as a whole.

Matters become tricky here as well, for several assumptions are operative for Gunkel that if removed may call the whole project into question. The first assumption is that genres in their original form were pure and simple; the second is that one must look for shared vocabulary and shared motifs common to these original forms; the third is that these original forms were located within a particular function or ceremony in Israel's corporate worship. Because the original form is the goal for Gunkel, then these presuppositions of his work, his bedrock, create the possibility of cutting and pasting the psalms as we have them now in their canonical shape. This is where form criticism meets redaction criticism, though Gunkel is not much interested in the latter and sees the redactional joining together of various psalm types as a hurdle to be overcome on the track to the original life setting.

The reader must remember that Gunkel is still after Israel's religion. There is a continuity in Gunkel's Old Testament work that covers his entire teaching and writing career, even though his attention is more directed at the literary aspects in his Psalms work. Still, Gunkel pursues the initial setting, a nonliterary setting, in Israel's worshiping life. Gunkel wants the psalms to function as a doorway to be walked through into the actual setting of Israel's "real life." In other words, "real life" is more important than Israel's literary life or canonical/scriptural life, and the latter serves the

---

67. Ibid., 15 – 16.

Old Testament scholar's real interest in the former. One senses this in the following comment from Gunkel:

> More important than all of this, however, is that by grouping the entire material by genres and motifs, we achieve firm standards that enable us to arrange the entire myriad *world of piety* expressed in the psalms according to their own disposition. We will find that the genres correspond to *religious types* that one can legitimately recognize. So from this point, all "biblical-theological" or, better, "religiohistorical" investigations treating the psalms that we do not wish to get lost in generalities must be based upon genre research.[68]

The forms or genres themselves provide the opportunity to enter into the real aim and intention of the interpreter, namely, Israel's ancient piety and religion.

The relationship between Israel's forms, as found in the psalms, and the original worship setting is a two-way street. The original worship setting sheds light on the psalm, and the psalm sheds light on the original worship setting. To Gunkel's mind, there were four basic original settings in Israel's worshiping life, and these settings correspond to Gunkel's primary genres as well. There was the *celebration of sacrifice*, the *lamentation of the community*, the *act of confession*, and the *thanksgiving offering of the pious individual*. These four settings correspond to the chief genres: *hymns, communal complaint songs, individual complaint songs*, and *individual songs of thanksgiving*.[69]

We begin to see the relationship between Gunkel's religious-historical instinct and his form-critical approach to the Psalter. They are organically related. Running the risk of oversimplification, Gunkel's form criticism is a two-step process. The genre of a particular psalm is identified as a means to enter into the multifunctional world of Israel's piety and religion in its earliest and purest form. By way of example, Gunkel's engagement with the genre of "hymns" leads to a section titled "The Religion of the Hymns."[70] The two-way relationship between form and worship setting when it comes to hymns has to do with Israel's ancient festivals, such as Rosh Hashanah, Passover, and Pentecost. From the hymn-psalms whose original setting was found in these particular aspects of Israel's worshiping life, we

---

68. Ibid., 18.
69. Ibid., 19.
70. Ibid., 47.

gain entry into religious expression of God's people in these ceremonies. Gunkel describes the religious-historical setting in terms of "fundamental moods." These fundamental moods on Israel's highest days of worship were *enthusiasm, adoration, reverence, praise,* and *exaltation.*[71] Here we have a prime example of how the forms of Israel's worship, now located in the literary deposit of the psalms, ultimately function for religious-historical reconstruction. In this reading, the Old Testament becomes a source for the reconstruction of not only the events of Israel's historical worship but also their religious sentiment, feelings, and moods.

Conclusion

Gunkel's form-critical reading of the psalms set a trajectory for Psalms research that continues to shape the discipline. No entry-level student who studies the Psalter walks away from class without some working knowledge of the various "categories" or genres of the psalms. Not everyone agrees with the particularities of Gunkel's form-critical understanding of the psalms. Sigmund Mowinckel, for example, charted a different course in his form-critical approach to the Psalter. For Mowinckel, Gunkel's form-critical analysis did not go far enough in making the connections between the psalms found in the Psalter and the cultic function of those psalms in the *Sitz im Leben* of Israel's worshiping life. "The majority of the extant psalms," says Mowinckel, "were in Gunkel's opinion no real cult psalms; they were 'spiritualized' imitations of the old, now mostly lost, cultic psalm poetry."[72] Gunkel's preference for the oral, preliterary stage of the psalms, according to Mowinckel, runs an unnecessary interference between the extant psalms and the real cultic situation that gave birth to the literary forms. Mowinckel retorts, "To this problem there is only one satisfying answer: the psalms are — with very few exceptions — real cult psalms, made for cultic use."[73] He also tinkers with Gunkel's sharp division between "I" psalms and "We" psalms, as Mowinckel claims to be correcting weaknesses in Gunkel's work by appealing to Gunkel's own fundamental insights — setting Gunkel over against Gunkel, so to speak in his project. Nevertheless, Mowinckel's course was made possible by Gunkel's early form-critical work.

---

71. Ibid.

72. Sigmund Mowinckel, *The Psalms in Israel's Worship*, trans. D. R. Ap-Thomas (Grand Rapids: Eerdmans, 2005), 29.

73. Ibid., 30.

The critical point to observe in Gunkel's project is his religious-historical endeavor to reconstruct Israel's experienced religion, including both the events and moods associated with these experiences. His form-critical approach is a means to this end. The final form and shape of the canonical documents are an impediment to be overcome in the tracing out of the earliest layers of Israel's traditions. More than this, however, is the loss of the canonical role the psalms continue to play in the shape and scope in which Judaism and Christianity have received them. On this account, the Bible is no longer an ongoing witness to divine revelation. It has become a source for the reconstruction of Israel's religion and a pathway to shared religious experiences with the divine.[74]

FOR FURTHER READING

Barton, John. *Reading the Old Testament: Method in Biblical Study.* Revised and Enlarged. Louisville: Westminster John Knox, 1996.

Berlin, Isaiah. *The Roots of Romanticism.* Princeton, N.J.: Princeton Univ. Press, 2001.

Childs, Brevard S. *Introduction to the Old Testament as Scripture.* Philadelphia: Fortress, 1979.

Clements, Ronald E. *A Century of Old Testament Study.* Cambridge, UK: Lutterworth, 1992.

Frei, Hans. *The Eclipse of Biblical Narrative: A Study in Eighteenth and Nineteenth Century Hermeneutics.* New Haven, Conn.: Yale Univ. Press, 1974.

Gunkel, Hermann. *Creation and Chaos in the Primeval Era and the Eschaton.* Translated by K. William Whitney Jr. Grand Rapids: Eerdmans, 2006.

———. *Genesis.* Translated by M. E. Biddle. Macon, Ga.: Mercer Univ. Press, 1997.

———. *Introduction to Psalms: The Genres of the Religious Lyric of Israel.* Translated by J. D. Nogalski. Macon, Ga.: Mercer Univ. Press, 1998.

continued on next page

---

74. The language of "source" and "witness" is taken from Brevard Childs (see, e.g., his *Biblical Theology of the Old and New Testaments: Theological Reflection on the Christian Bible* [Minneapolis: Fortress, 1992], 144).

Knight, Douglas A. *Rediscovering the Traditions of Israel*. 3rd edition. Studies in Biblical Literature. Atlanta: Society of Biblical Literature, 2006.

O'Neill, J. C. *The Bible's Authority: A Portrait Gallery of Thinkers from Lessing to Bultmann*. Edinburgh: T&T Clark, 1991.

Smend, Rudolf. *From Astruc to Zimmerli: Old Testament Scholarship in Three Centuries*. Translated by M. Kohl. Tübingen: Mohr Siebeck, 2007.

Tucker, Gene M. *Form Criticism of the Old Testament*. Philadelphia: Fortress, 1971.

Gerhard von Rad

(1901–1971)

The Old Testament's Living Traditions

Gerhard von Rad died on Reformation Day in 1971. Appropriately, the lectionary reading for the day was Hebrews 13:7: "Remember your leaders, those who spoke to you the word of God; consider the outcome of their life, and imitate their faith."[1] Von Rad's exegetical and theological work on the Old Testament created a horizon of interest and further study of the subject matter whose impact is felt to this day. He was a teacher. Reflecting on his teaching life, von Rad states, "My task as an academic teacher was and is: read to learn and read to teach."[2] For many, he was their teacher who spoke the word of God in the Old Testament to them; Walther Zimmerli, Rolf Rendtorff, James Crenshaw, and Brevard Childs — all standard names in Old Testament scholarship — were shaped by von Rad's exegetical vision. However one receives his tradition-historical approach to Old Testament exegesis or his formal wedding of those reconstructions to the task of Old Testament theology proper, denying or avoiding the importance of von Rad in the history of Old Testament interpretation is not an option. As a teacher of mine once said in passing, "We can pick at von Rad's Old Testament theology all we want, but the car had wheels on it and was driving around the block." Certainly, this is true.

---

1. Rudolf Smend notes this peculiar providence (*From Astruc to Zimmerli: Old Testament Scholarship in Three Centuries*, trans. M. Kohl [Tübingen: Mohr Siebeck, 2007], 197).

2. "Meine Aufgabe als akademischer Lehrer war und ist: lesen zu lernen und lesen zu lehrnen" (*Gottes Wirken in Israel: Vorträge zum Alten Testament* [Neukirchen-Vluyn: Neukirchener Verlag des Erziehungsvereins, 1974], 321).

As is our custom, we will look briefly at von Rad's life and intellectual setting and then lay out the major contours of his Old Testament interpretation.

Von Rad's Life and Early Twentieth Century Context

Von Rad was a complex and full personality whose influence on Old Testament scholarship both in Europe and North America is wide-ranging. Rudolf Smend describes von Rad's lectures in Göttingen and Heidelberg as "places of pilgrimage."[3] His spoken and written work had a "spellbinding" effect on listeners and readers.[4] Norman Porteous, a contemporary of von Rad at the University of Edinburgh, warns, "So brilliant and persuasive is the writing, that one can be pardoned if at times one's critical faculty is lulled to sleep."[5] Von Rad captured the Old Testament imagination of an entire generation. When the Old Testament rose from its dormant status after World War II, von Rad's theological vision of the Old Testament shaped the horizon of anticipation for many. One probable reason is the connection between von Rad's identity as professor and preacher. Von Rad was a man of the academy. But he was also a man for the church. Von Rad's Old Testament studies were not a detached academic exercise. He studied and taught the Old Testament as one listening for the Word of God in the traditions of Israel's scriptural legacy.[6]

Firsthand accounts of von Rad reveal a multifaceted and interesting character. He had a strong sense of familial tradition (a term that later takes material form in his Old Testament interpretation). He was a lover of music who played the violin. He read German literature feverishly and thoroughly. His intellectual and cultural interests were round and full. In a review of James Crenshaw's *Gerhard von Rad*, Brevard Childs laments the volume:

> Probably those scholars who were privileged to know von Rad personally will come away with some feeling of incompleteness. The full

---

3. Smend, *From Astruc to Zimmerli*, 170.

4. Ibid.

5. Quoted in ibid.

6. It is the lack of this energetic combination that some critique in the heirs of von Rad. For example, Joseph Groves finds the tradition-critical work of Odil Steck, a student of von Rad, lacking because of its desire for precision and absence of theological energy that pervades the work of von Rad (*Actualization and Interpretation in the Old Testament* [Society of Biblical Literature Dissertation Series 86; Atlanta: Scholars Press, 1987], 99).

dimension of his unusual personality tends to get lost in the description of his work. One senses little of his sense of humor, the significant role of music in his life, and the nature of his theological passion.[7]

Childs's larger point is that "the various sides of his genius" so intertwined as to make a stripped-down sketch of von Rad too flat a portrait.

Von Rad was born on October 21, 1901, in Nuremberg. He was a German southerner who spent his formative years in this region and, as providence would have it, died in the southern town of Heidelberg. His father was a psychiatrist from the nobility of Augsburg, though the status of this pedigree did not infect von Rad. His early years were principally shaped by his mother. Smend describes her as a "vivacious woman with a fund of wisdom, talented with her pen and a gifted musician."[8] Music and words were central to von Rad's early development, with his mother playing the lead role.

Von Rad struggled in school as a young man. Though charming and gifted in speech, von Rad found arithmetic difficult. His academic struggles mounted to such a degree that he was sent to a boarding school so he could pass his examinations. Unfortunately, von Rad's academic struggles continued in boarding school until a new headmaster encouraged him in his studies, possibly expanding his knowledge of the literature of the day. The headmaster announced hopefully to his mother, "He will surprise you yet!"[9] The headmaster's announcement proved prophetic.

Theology was not a likely choice of academic study for von Rad. What was said of Dietrich Bonhoeffer (someone von Rad knew since childhood), Rudolf Smend applies to von Rad: "It was extremely rare for a young man belonging to this upper academic class to decide for theology."[10] Von Rad's first academic and vocational choice was medicine, but his father thought his personal constitution unsuited for such a pursuit. Von Rad was left with a choice between classics and theology. His eventual choice for theology was in large measure due to the influence of his pastor, Wilhelm Stählin. In 1916, Stählin became pastor of St. Lorenz in Nuremberg. During his tenure as pastor of St. Lorenz, he led a small group study of Karl Barth's newly published *Epistle to the Romans* (1919). Von Rad attended this Wednesday study group and would later call himself "a member of 'the

---

7. Brevard S. Childs, "Review of *Gerhard von Rad*, by James L. Crenshaw," *Journal of Biblical Literature* 100 (1981): 460.
8. Smend, *From Astruc to Zimmerli*, 173.
9. Ibid.
10. Ibid.

Epistle to the Romans generation.' "[11] Stählin's influence on young von Rad and the force of Barth's theological exegesis of Romans cast the die for the young man. He turned his attention decidedly to theology.

Von Rad studied theology from 1921 – 1925. The first and last years of his academic studies took place at Erlangen University, with the middle years at the University of Tübingen. These were tumultuous years in the German church. The struggle for the Old Testament was in the middle of the fray. In 1921, the *Bund für Deutsche Kirche* (League of German Churches) was organized in Berlin. This grassroots organization published a biannual journal, *The German Church*, which espoused heavily anti-Semitic and anti-Old Testament sentiments. With the ascendancy of National Socialism (Nazis) on the horizon, these anti-Semitic instincts would eventually dominate the German national church. Alongside this anti-Semitic rhetoric was a deep-seated distrust and dislike of the Old Testament. To state the obvious, the Old Testament was too Jewish. The general tenor of von Rad's entire scholarly career, especially during the prewar and war years, was a strong no to these anti-Semitic and anti-Old Testament ideas.

After serving several congregations as a curate and vicar, von Rad turned his attention to the completion of his doctoral dissertation during his free year of study, 1927 – 1928.[12] His doctoral supervisor, Professor Otto Procksch, suggested the subject of von Rad's dissertation, "The People of God in Deuteronomy." In this work, von Rad's interest in the theology of the Old Testament was already present. He determined to engage Deuteronomy in its own literary form from within. Von Rad's interest was in understanding Deuteronomy as a theological whole, though he was fully aware of the complex comingling of Israel's traditions in the final form of the text. Many themes that von Rad would later explore more fully were present in this early work.

Otto Procksch would send his best students to further their studies under his friend Albrecht Alt in Leipzig.[13] Von Rad was one of those stu-

---

11. Ibid.; see pp. 173 – 74 for more regarding the "curious paradox" of Stählin's introducing Barth to von Rad and the eventual struggle between Stählin and Barth at the University of Münster.

12. Manfred Oeming, "Gerhard von Rad as a Theologian of the Church," *Interpretation* 62 (2008): 232; Smend, *From Astruc to Zimmerli*, 174.

13. Albrecht Alt's historical work on the Old Testament opened up new avenues for understanding the early history of Israel, especially in his presentation of the early settlement in Palestine. Alt's form-critical skills made use of Israel's traditions to measure the historicity of the biblical material. For an overview of Alt's approach and his role in the burgeoning field of tradition-criticism, see

dents, and in 1930, he wrote his second dissertation (*Habilitationsschrift*) on the nature of history in the Chronicler under Alt's tutelage.[14] During the years 1930 – 1934, von Rad worked as an associate of Alt. The position was left vacant by his other star pupil, Martin Noth. Alt's influence on von Rad was significant. In von Rad's installation lecture at the University of Heidelberg some years later, he said of Alt, "I count it as one of the most fortunate leadings of my life that this scholar and incomparable teacher put up with me for four years as his assistant and lecturer, never ceasing to encourage me; and that I was permitted to retain my ties with him, professionally and personally, until his death."[15]

During these years as Alt's assistant, von Rad's scholarly output was prodigious. He published a third monograph on the Priestly writer in the Hexateuch, as well as several substantial articles and dictionary entries, e.g., the Old Testament background sections for *angelos* and *basileus* in Kittel's *Theological Dictionary of the New Testament*.[16] As a nonstipendiary lecturer, von Rad had to lecture and was responsible for the offered Hebrew course. Von Rad kept busy during these years. At the same time, he was proving himself as a burgeoning scholar who was already leaving his mark on the discipline. Though von Rad was only thirty-three years old, it came as no surprise that in 1934 he was offered a professor's chair at the University of Jena. He occupied this chair until he was forced into military service in 1944.

These years in Jena were momentous, not only for von Rad's scholarly vocation, but also for the events about to engulf the whole world. The University of Jena was in the Thuringia region of East Germany. Thuringia became strongly pro-Nazi as National Socialist ideology and propaganda placed a stranglehold on the university and the Protestant church in this region. In retrospect, we see von Rad's great courage in the face of this rising opposition to the truth of the gospel and the central role the Old

---

Douglas A. Knight, *Rediscovering the Traditions of Israel*, 3rd ed. (Studies in Biblical Literature; Atlanta: Society of Biblical Literature, 2006), 73 – 76.

14. In the German university system, a second dissertation is required to teach at the university level. These dissertations were more modest in scope and size than is most often associated with doctoral dissertations today. One recalls that de Wette's dissertation was only sixteen pages in length!

15. Von Rad, *Gottes Wirken in Israel*, 318. On the important, even if professional, relationship between von Rad and Alt, see Smend, *From Astruc to Zimmerli*, 176 – 78.

16. The monograph was titled *Die Priesterschrift im Hexateuch. Literarisch untersucht und theologisch gewertet* (Beiträge zur Wissenschaft vom Alter und Neuen Testament; Stuttgart: Kohlhammer, 1934).

Testament plays in it. He aligned himself with the Confessing Church (*Bekennende Kirche*) over against the pro-Hitler German Christians (*Deutsche Christen*). Von Rad's name was in the mix of other well-known members such as Karl Barth, Dietrich Bonhoeffer, and Wilhelm Vischer.

The Barmen Declaration was the confessional statement of the Confessing Church. This statement, written primarily by Karl Barth in May of 1934, confessed unreserved allegiance to Jesus Christ who is witnessed to in Holy Scriptures as the foundation and Lord of the church.[17] The statement took direct aim at the German Christians' oath of allegiance to Hitler as the leader (*Führer*) of the church. Only Jesus is the *Führer* of the church, the ecclesiology of Barmen declares. The stakes associated with such a robust commitment to the supremacy and sufficiency of Jesus Christ and the Holy Scriptures, both Old Testament and New Testament, were high. Von Rad's physical placement at pro-Nazi Jena made the stakes even higher.

Bernard Levinson's article, "Reading the Bible in Nazi Germany," is an engaging and moving account of von Rad's tenure at Jena during the Nazi maelstrom.[18] Levinson suggests von Rad's particular understanding of Deuteronomy as a text emphasizing the grace of God (gospel) over against an overly legal reading of the book was not a purely exegetical conclusion; in fact, such exegetical conclusions, according to Levinson, require some nifty footwork in light of the straightforward claims of certain sections in Deuteronomy. In retrospect, it becomes clearer that von Rad's theological account of Deuteronomy was heavily influenced by his particular social/historical setting. His exegesis of Deuteronomy was a subversive statement against National Socialist ideology.[19]

Von Rad's exegesis of Deuteronomy was a concerted effort to demonstrate the Old Testament's continuing canonical role as Christian Scrip-

---

17. Article 1 of the Barmen Declaration states, "The impregnable foundation of the German Evangelical Church is the Gospel of Jesus Christ, as it is revealed in Holy Scripture and came again to the light in the creeds of the Reformation. In this way the authorities, which the church needs for her mission, are defined and limited" (quoted in John H. Leith, ed., *Creeds of the Churches: A Reader in Christian Doctrine, from the Bible to the Present* [Atlanta: John Knox Press, 1982], 518; see also Eberhard Busch, *The Barmen Theses Then and Now*, trans. D. Guder and J. Guder (Grand Rapids: Eerdmans, 2010).

18. Bernard M. Levinson, "Reading the Bible in Nazi Germany: Gerhard von Rad's Attempt to Reclaim the Old Testament for the Church," *Interpretation* 62 (2008): 238 – 54.

19. Ibid., 240; Levinson notes approvingly Walter Brueggemann's and Jean-Louis Ska's respective statements regarding von Rad's understanding of salvation history as a polemic against Nazi ideology.

ture. This interpretive move stood in opposition to the German Christians' attempt to de-Judaize the church, which rejected the church's confession regarding the canonical status of the Old Testament. The neo-Marcionite tendencies in Friedrich Schleiermacher's theology of the nineteenth century and in Adolf von Harnack's historical theology of the early twentieth century made for a noxious combination when mingled with Nazi ideology.[20] Anti-Semitism and anti-Old Testament sentiments were viewed as flip sides of the same coin. In 1933, German Christian leader Dr. Reinhold Krause encouraged the German church to align itself more with Nazi ideology by dispersing itself of anything "Un-German in worship and confession; liberation from the Old Testament with its Jewish morality of profit and its stories of cattle traders and pimps."[21] Von Rad devoted himself to the Christian study of the Old Testament in this ideological context. Few university settings proved more challenging for advancing such research and teaching than Jena.

The University of Jena was at the forefront of Nazi infiltration into the intellectual life of Germany. Levinson recounts Wolfgang Meyer's fascinating rise to power in the ranks of Jena's university life. Meyer, who changed his name to Meyer-Erlach lest he be thought a Jew, was appointed to the chair of practical theology with neither his doctorate nor habilitation. A year after his initial appointment, he was made dean of the theology faculty. In another year (1935), he was made rector of the university. Levinson recounts Meyer-Erlach having only eight of the 129 faculty votes when appointed rector.[22] How von Rad actually came to a chair in the heavily politicized University of Jena is nothing other than a stroke of bizarre providence. Levinson believes von Rad's appointment only took place because of his relationship with Gerhard Kittel, a longtime devotee of National Socialism, alongside the fact that the University of Jena did not do their homework on von Rad. Levinson surmises, "In any case, even before he went to Jena, von Rad was giving public lectures stressing that there is no access to Christ except through the OT. Had this material been read, it is hard to imagine that he would have been appointed."[23]

---

20. In a celebrated work on Marcion, von Harnack claims that the early church rightly rejected Marcion's insistence on doing away with the Old Testament. But it was only a weakness of knee that kept the church of the twentieth century from removing the canonical status of the Old Testament (*Marcion: The Gospel of the Alien God*, trans. John E. Seeley and Lyle D. Bierma [Durham: Labyrinth, 1990]).

21. Quoted in Levinson, "Reading the Bible in Nazi Germany," 241.

22. Levinson, "Reading the Bible in Nazi Germany," 243.

23. Ibid., 244.

The signs of Nazi influence on the theology faculty were evident. The University of Jena was the first theology faculty to remove its required Hebrew course for students. Von Rad resisted this move, but with the retirement of his ally, Waldemar Macholz, chair of ecumenical studies, he was a lone voice of opposition.[24] Von Rad's isolation at the university continued. According to the records of the winter semester 1935–1936, 155 students were enrolled in the theology faculty. In his Psalms course he had four students, with only two students in his courses on Jeremiah and Deutero-Isaiah. Levenson tells that by the winter semester 1941–1942, enrollment in the entire theology faculty had dwindled to ten.[25] As it is told, the Confessing Church sent students to Jena for the express purpose of filling von Rad's classroom with some students. Otherwise, von Rad feared, the university would shut down the entire theology faculty.[26] Levinson rounds out the description of von Rad's isolation during these days by stating, "Most indicative of his academic isolation is the fact that not a single one of the forty-five doctoral dissertations submitted to the faculty of theology during his tenure at Jena was directed by von Rad."[27] It is difficult at this point not to conceive of von Rad's scholarly life and struggle for the Old Testament in the Christian church as von Rad *contra mundum*.[28] It was, in fact, von Rad, amid many other faithful voices, who spoke out for the lordship of Jesus Christ and the authority of the Scriptures, both Old and New Testaments, in the church.

In the summer of 1944, von Rad was forced into military service.[29] During his short stint in military service, von Rad wrote his family: "I can only fall back on the very simple resignation of Paul Gerhardt's hymn, 'I have put my heart and mind in the heart and mind of God.' For, after all, that is unshakeable. Of course I don't mean to say that I am not continually plagued by a great despair."[30] Then in March of 1945, just a little over a month before the end of the European front of the war, von Rad

---

24. Ibid.

25. Ibid., 246.

26. Ibid.

27. Ibid.

28. For further particulars on how von Rad executed his theological vision for the Old Testament while at Jena, see Levinson, "Reading the Bible in Nazi Germany," 246–48; see also Smend, *From Astruc to Zimmerli*, 179–80.

29. For further particulars on von Rad's military service, see Smend, *From Astruc to Zimmerli*, 184–85.

30. Quoted in Smend, *From Astruc to Zimmerli*, 184–85.

was taken as a prisoner of war by the Americans at Bad Kreusnach.[31] He remained a prisoner of war until the end of June but suffered the effects of malnutrition for years.[32] Von Rad's days as a prisoner of war were a time of extreme difficulty.[33] He described the situation in terms of a God-forsakenness of biblical proportions.[34] Even in these dire straits, von Rad remained the teacher, lecturing to the prisoners on the book of Genesis. He also remained the minister as he encouraged young theologians in their faith, preached to the prisoners, and administered the sacraments.

After the trauma of the war, von Rad lectured at several institutions before moving in late 1945 to a permanent post at the University of Göttingen. Providence now smiled on von Rad. On the far side of the war's damaging effects, students and teachers in the theology faculty at Göttingen were bound together in a most special way. Smend recounts few teachers at Göttingen having a more profound impact on the students than von Rad.[35] His lecture halls were filled to overflowing. During his tenure at Wellhausen's old stomping ground, a fact of which von Rad was keenly aware, he kept a breakneck pace. He lectured early in the morning, offered other lectures as well, attended and ran seminars, all while maintaining an aggressive research agenda. "Von Rad," Smend reveals, "never of robust health and, like most people, weakened by the deprivation of those years, was stretched to the limits of his strength."[36] During these years, he continued to pursue his special interest in Deuteronomy.

In 1949, von Rad took an Old Testament chair at the University of Heidelberg. Heidelberg was especially suited to von Rad, and he remained there for the rest of his life. As one would expect, von Rad was especially productive during his time at Heidelberg. He published his famous commentary on Genesis and his two-volume *Theology of the Old Testament*, to name a few of many. But we would be remiss if we did not take note of von Rad's deep love for the church and his continued service to her. Von Rad was a professor *and* a preacher. Smend describes von Rad as "a passionate preacher and a passionate listener to sermons."[37] He never approached the

---

31. James L. Crenshaw, *Gerhard von Rad* (Waco, Tex.: Word, 1978), 24.
32. Ibid.
33. Ibid., 24–25.
34. Smend, *From Astruc to Zimmerli*, 185.
35. Ibid., 187.
36. Ibid., 186.
37. Ibid., 196. Smend recounts von Rad's approval of Gerhard Ebeling's statement, "The criterion of theology is preaching." Von Rad added, "That has accompanied me."

academic study of the Old Testament in isolation from his identity as a Christian and churchman. Manfred Oeming confirms this in the following: "For von Rad, proclamation of God's word to the congregation was the true goal of his scholarly work."[38] Von Rad preached regularly in the services of St. Peter's Church in Heidelberg. Oeming describes von Rad's sermons there as "the stuff of legends."[39]

We will engage von Rad's particular tradition-historical approach to Old Testament interpretation in the section to follow. It should be stated on the front end that many of von Rad's exegetical and theological conclusions have been called into question. Nevertheless, von Rad was a multifaceted character whose impact on Old Testament interpretation will be felt for generations. Von Rad was a teacher, preacher, and scholar. Each of these facets of his life mutually informed the other, making von Rad the theologian he was.

Von Rad and the Traditions of Israel

During his Jena days (1938), von Rad published a fourth monograph considered by many, including von Rad himself, to be his most important contribution to the field of Old Testament criticism.[40] The title of the short monograph was *The Form-Critical Problem of the Hexateuch*. We will focus primarily on this work of von Rad because in many ways it shaped the trajectory for his approach to Old Testament exegesis, history, and theology. I also recognize this is a limited reading of von Rad, especially when he is best known for his Old Testament theology.

It is impossible to understand von Rad's approach to Old Testament studies without a thorough appreciation of its form-critical roots. In fact, von Rad would at times tell his students that he had "Gunkel's blood" running through his veins.[41] In the previous chapter, we observed Gunkel's approach to the literature of the Old Testament as a species of form criticism par excellence. The present literary shape of biblical books or larger parts of the canonical whole, e.g., the Psalms or the Torah, became

---

38. Oeming, "Gerhard von Rad as a Theologian of the Church," 236.

39. Ibid. On the significance of preaching in von Rad's theology, see Martin Hauger, "'But We Were in the Wilderness, and There God Speaks Quite Differently': On the Significance of Preaching in the Theology of Gerhard von Rad," *Interpretation* 62 (2008): 278 – 92.

40. See Smend, *From Astruc to Zimmerli*, 182.

41. Rolf Rendtorff, *Canon and Theology: Overtures to an Old Testament Theology*, trans. Margaret Kohl (Overtures to Biblical Theology; Minneapolis: Fortress, 1993), 209.

a source for the critical retrieval and reconstruction of Israel's religious life. The Pentateuch, or Hexateuch as von Rad understood it (the five books of Moses plus Joshua), is a complex amalgamation of various religious traditions that once stood independently from one another. By means of analyzing the various genres according to their content, religious expression, and *Sitz im Leben*, the form critic reconstructs the religious outlook of Israel in her historical past. Gunkel's approach isolated Israel's traditions as he moved away from the final form of the text, e.g., the Pentateuch as a whole, to the identification of these traditions in their oral prehistory — "he spoke of scenes around the campfires and of professional storytellers."[42] This was the scene Gunkel attempted to reconstruct. Regarding the canonical shape of the material, Gunkel states matter-of-factly, "The spirit loses power. The genres are exhausted; imitations begin to abound. Redactions take the place of original creations ... Finally, the canon took shape."[43] The move from oral history to written history was a "tragedy" for Gunkel.

Von Rad's tradition-historical approach breathes the air of form criticism and its tendency to isolate Israel's independent traditions. Where Gunkel's focus tended toward Israel's oral religious history, von Rad's interest was in the final form of the Hexateuch and the long, complicated road leading to this final form. The final form of the Hexateuch served as a window into the various layers of tradition now brought together in the final literary unit.[44] How did the Hexateuch come to its current form and shape when embedded within it are various and competing traditions of Israel's past? Answering this question was at the center of von Rad's critical investigation. Or as Douglas Knight frames the issue, "What von Rad ... did was to start with the most ancient confessional beliefs found in the Old Testament and, using these as the key, to try to explain the compositional form of the Hexateuch *as a whole* in light of its feasible course of development stretching from the originally separate traditions on to their final form in the present context."[45]

Though it may be too simplistic a formula in light of the complexity

---

42. John H. Hayes and Frederick Prussner, *Old Testament Theology: Its History and Development* (Atlanta: John Knox Press, 1985), 235.

43. Hermann Gunkel, *Water for a Thirsty Land: Israelite Literature and Religion*, ed. K. C. Hanson (Minneapolis: Fortress, 2001), 36.

44. Gerhard von Rad, "The Form-Critical Problem of the Hexateuch," in *From Genesis to Chronicles: Explorations in Old Testament Theology*, trans. E. W. T. Dicken (Minneapolis: Fortress, 2005), 1–2.

45. Knight, *Rediscovering the Traditions of Israel*, 78.

and depth of Gunkel's and von Rad's work, their respective and overlapping approaches might be summarized as follows: Gunkel moved backward in the isolation of traditions and forms in the Old Testament to the original situation in Israel's religious and cultic life — campfires, storytellers, and temple cult — whereas von Rad's form criticism allowed the isolation of the disparate traditions embedded in the Hexateuch to provide the key for unlocking the forward movement of Israel's salvation history and literary development in the Hexateuch. Von Rad's tradition criticism was a form-critical enterprise that allowed the final form of the Hexateuch to reveal the various layers of once independent traditions now on their way to being situated next to each other in the final literary form of the Hexateuch. The final form in this tradition-critical approach is not necessarily valued any more than the other layers of tradition. In fact, the final form of the Hexateuch is simply the final stage in a complex literary history of growth. To summarize, von Rad's tradition-critical approach to Israel's confessional life emphasizes the actualization of Israel's ancient traditions again and again in her life of faith — *Vergegenwärtigung* (actualization), a term von Rad employs to reveal the dynamic and continual reception of Israel's traditions.[46]

Von Rad's thesis begins with an analysis of three "little historical creeds" (*kleines geschichtliches Credo*) embedded within the final form of the Hexateuch. By means of form-critical investigation, these three little credos open a window into Israel's early cultic life and Israel's own understanding of their salvation history. The three confessions of faith are Deuteronomy 26:5b – 9; Deuteronomy 6:20 – 24; and Joshua 24:2b – 13. The first credo is representative of the form of all three. Deuteronomy 26:5b – 9 confesses:

> "My father was a wandering Aramean, and he went down into Egypt with a few people and lived there and became a great nation, powerful and numerous. But the Egyptians mistreated us and made us suffer, subjecting us to hard labor. Then we cried out to the LORD, the God of our ancestors, and the LORD heard our voice and saw our misery, toil and oppression. So the LORD brought us out of Egypt with a mighty hand and an outstretched arm, with great terror and with signs and wonders. He brought us to this place and gave us this land, a land flowing with milk and honey."

---

46. See especially Groves, *Actualization and Interpretation in the Old Testament.*

For von Rad, "There can, however, be no possible doubt that this speech is not an *ad hoc* composition."[47] Rather, these three confessions of faith reveal ancient Israel's cultic life and credo concerning her history of redemption. Because they share a common literary form, it follows that they share a common tradition received from Israel's ancient past — again, von Rad's indebtedness to form criticism's basic procedures is observed. These credo statements are short (revealing their antiquity), exalted in form, and lacking any reference to the events of Sinai, a feature which is important to von Rad's subsequent tradition-historical analysis.[48] From these observations, von Rad concludes, "Surely then it is not unduly bold to conclude that the solemn recital of the main parts of the redemptive narrative must have been an invariable feature of the ancient Israelite cultus, either as a straightforward creedal statement or as a hortatory address to the congregation."[49] This particular tradition represented in these three credos is called the "settlement tradition" by von Rad and can be traced in other places in the Old Testament as well, e.g., Psalm 136, Judges, the song of Moses at the Red Sea (Exodus 15). There is a fixity to these literary types, revealing the fixity and independent nature of this particular settlement tradition in Israel's ancient worshiping life. With time, the bare bones of this settlement tradition may allow a flexibility to its fixity, with secondary reminiscences added later — election, worship of the high places, the rejection of Shiloh, Mount Zion — still, the settlement tradition is by and large absent of any presence of the Sinai tradition.[50]

Once the independence and flexibility of the settlement tradition is explored, von Rad then analyzes the other dominant tradition in the Hexateuch, namely, the Sinai tradition. The tension between the traditions, according to von Rad (and instigated by Wellhausen), is observed in the settlement tradition's narrative portrayal of Israel's immediate movement into Kadesh, the goal of their journey, right after the deliverance from the Red Sea. There is no excursion to Sinai in the settlement tradition's account of things (Exodus 17) — whereas the Sinai tradition observed in

---

47. Von Rad, "Form-Critical Problem," 6.

48. Ibid., 6–7.

49. Ibid., 6.

50. Von Rad writes, "We may sum up the result of our enquiry in the following way: even the more or less free accounts of the redemptive-story which follow the canonical scheme do not mention the events of Sinai. These events seem rather to have given rise to a tradition of their own, which remained separate from the canonical pattern and only at a very late date became combined with it" ("Form-Critical Problem," 10).

Exodus 19 – 24 and 32 – 34 takes Israel on an excursion to Sinai that is "unheard of" in the settlement tradition.[51] Again, this provides strong evidence for von Rad's insistence on the independence of these two traditions. The shape of von Rad's approach to the traditions of Israel is beginning to peek through. The Sinai tradition, in distinction from the settlement tradition, is concerned with two dominant matters: the theophany at Mount Sinai and the making of the covenant. Other traditional elements eventually attached themselves to the Sinai material. But at its core, the Sinai tradition was concerned primarily with these two matters.[52]

The discrete traditions may be characterized as follows: The settlement tradition focused on God's redemptive-historical guidance of his people to the Promised Land, whereas the Sinai tradition focused on the coming of God to his people in a momentous act of revelation.[53] Von Rad does not labor over which tradition is more historically credible than the other. Such a question is inappropriate for him in light of the kind of material he believes the Hexateuch is — a retelling of Israel's history from the perspective of their faith, not an empirical history of what really happened. Rather, the question von Rad pursues is what "particular place and function" these two traditions had in Israel's religious life.[54] Here we see the organic relationship of form criticism to tradition criticism in von Rad's larger historical-critical project. The Hexateuchal traditions do not give us a historical account of Israel that will satisfy modern attempts at history making. What these traditions do give is insight into Israel's ancient faith and how that faith was continually actualized in Israel's history of salvation.

As a result of von Rad's tradition-historical inquiry, he concludes that the Hexateuch in its final form has brought together two once independent traditions: the settlement and the Sinai traditions.[55] But who brought together these discrete traditions along with the various traditional accou-

---

51. Ibid., 11.
52. Ibid., 14.
53. Ibid., 15 – 16.
54. Ibid., 16. Von Rad spends the next twenty pages exploring the cultic *Sitz im Leben* of these two independent traditions. In short, the settlement/exodus tradition was associated with the Festival of Weeks celebrated at the ancient shrine of Gilgal. The Sinai tradition's original cultic setting was the Feast of Tabernacles celebrated at Shechem (see Hayes and Prussner, *Old Testament Theology*, 236).
55. In the footnotes, Douglas Knight (*Rediscovering the Traditions of Israel*, 82) refers to John Bright's (the English translator of von Rad's *Old Testament Theology*) and A. S. van der Woude's respective statements regarding von Rad's argument from silence in his analysis of these traditions in the cultic life of Israel.

trements now attached to them? Here von Rad introduces Israel's first and greatest theologian — the Yahwist.

Von Rad challenged Gunkel's understanding of the redaction history of the Pentateuch. For Gunkel, the Yahwist was more a collector than an author; that is, the Yahwist was a more passive agent whose role was like an archivist rather than a theologian or author. Von Rad dismisses this notion. In fact, the Yahwist, according to von Rad, is the creator of the Hexateuch. It was the Yahwist, who in the height of the Solomonic era, produced this work and in this sense is the author of the Hexateuch.[56]

What, in fact, did the Yahwist do? He placed the Sinai tradition between the settlement tradition's account of the exodus and entry into the land. The Yahwist expanded Israel's patriarchal history and prefixed it to this newly fitted settlement/Sinai complex. He also affixed the primeval history (found in Genesis 1 – 11) to the patriarchal history. In other words, none of these various independent traditions of Israel were received whole hog by the Yahwist. They were all refitted and reworked into an organic whole whose overarching theological vision had to do with "a history of divine providence and guidance."[57]

Von Rad summarizes his understanding of the Yahwist, "If therefore we think of the J writer as being by no means wholly dependent upon what had gone before, either with regard to the literary form of his work or to the materials he brought together, we can yet scarcely overestimate his contribution in shaping the material, and in directing the theological motivation which runs through it."[58] The literary achievement of the Yahwist is an enormous feat within Israel's religious life and a testimony to his theological genius. Even though the Hexateuch's compositional history is not completed with the Yahwist's work, "the form of the Hexateuch had already been finally determined by the Yahwist."[59] The later work of the Elohist and Priestly writers "are no more than variations upon the massive theme of the Yahwist's conception, despite their admittedly great theological originality."[60] Who is essentially responsible for Israel's

---

56. Von Rad, "Form-Critical Problem," 51.

57. Smend, *From Astruc to Zimmerli*, 47.

58. Von Rad, "Form-Critical Problem," 47. See Thomas Römer's helpful history of Pentateuchal research in Thomas B. Dozeman and Konrad Schmid, eds., *A Farewell to the Yahwist? The Composition of the Pentateuch in Recent European Interpretation* (Society of Biblical Literature Symposium Series 34; Atlanta: Society of Biblical Literature, 2006), 9 – 27, esp. 16.

59. Von Rad, "Form-Critical Problem," 55.

60. Ibid.

and the church's Pentateuch (or Hexateuch)? For von Rad, the answer is unambiguously straightforward: the Yahwist is.

In summary, what did the Yahwist do as the creator of the Hexateuch? We will allow von Rad to answer this question:

> (1) The extensive development of the original creedal deposit. (2) An internal ordering and arrangement of the saga material, so that Yahweh's guidance is manifest both in isolated instances and in the work as a whole. (3) The integration of the saga material into the traditional notion of the God of the patriarchs, and his promise of the land. (4) The reorientation of the patriarchal sagas, which now become introduction to the settlement tradition, to which they now stand in the relationship of a promise which it fulfills. (5) The relating of the patriarchal covenant to the Sinai covenant, similarly conceived as promise and fulfillment.[61]

These five matters reveal the theological outlook and literary achievement of Israel's greatest theologian.[62]

Von Rad's conclusion to "The Form-Critical Problem of the Hexateuch" is an important statement regarding his understanding of tradition history and its relation to the final form of the canonical text.

> No doubt the Hexateuch in its complete and final form makes great demands upon the understanding of its readers. Many ages, many men, many traditions, and many theologians have contributed to this stupendous work. The Hexateuch will be rightly understood, therefore, not by those who read it superficially, but only by those who study it with a knowledge of its profundities, recognizing that its pages speak of the revelations and religious experiences of many different periods. *None of the stages in the age-long development of this work have been wholly superseded; something has been preserved of each phase, and its influence has persisted right down to the final form of the Hexateuch.* Only a recognition of this fact can prepare one to hear the plenitude of the witness which this work encompasses.[63]

---

61. Ibid., 47.

62. Von Rad's valorizing of the Yahwist has come under critical scrutiny, most importantly from his student Rolf Rendtorff (see Rendtorff, *The Problem of the Process of Transmission in the Pentateuch*, trans. John J. Scullion [Journal for the Study of the Old Testament: Supplement Series; Sheffield: JSOT, 1990]).

63. Von Rad, "Form-Critical Problem," 58, emphasis his.

Von Rad's conclusion is clear: The final form of the Pentateuch (Hexateuch) is the final stage in a long history of reception and actualization of Israel's ancient and various traditions. An appreciation and recognition of the Pentateuch's depth dimension is necessary for proper reading and interpretation. *Moreover, equal emphasis should be placed on the various layers of tradition (along with the revelations and religious experiences out of which those traditions arose) and the final form of the canonical document.* The final form of the Hexateuch is the final stage of Israel's literary actualization of her past traditions. It is afforded no more priority than the previous stages embedded in the Hexateuch.

A central claim of von Rad is that a proper understanding and reception of the Pentateuch demands an appreciative reception and investigation into the various traditions that lay behind the present form of the material.[64] The conjoining of a forward-moving salvation history within a tradition-critical approach defined by actualization forms the framework for much of von Rad's subsequent work, e.g., *Old Testament Theology*, and the typological relationship of the Old Testament to the New Testament.

Von Rad's *Old Testament Theology*: A Brief Reflection

The scope of von Rad's work goes far beyond his early monograph on form-critical problems in the Hexateuch. Without a doubt, he is most remembered for his two volumes on Old Testament theology. These two volumes are a high-water mark of Old Testament theology in the twentieth century. That von Rad is primarily remembered for them is surely right. John Hayes and Frederick Prussner describe these volumes as the inauguration of "a new epoch in the study of Old Testament theology."[65] Detailed attention to von Rad's magnum opus will take us too far afield. But a few comments should be made in light of the investigation above into his critical work on the Hexateuch.

For von Rad, a proper Old Testament theology should resist two tendencies: (1) the danger of confusing Israel's own account of her history with Israel's actual, empirical history and (2) a misguided attempt at making the

---

64. This historical-critical instinct shaped von Rad's strong resistance to Wilhelm Vischer's approach to reading the Old Testament Christianly.

65. Hayes and Prussner, *Old Testament Theology*, 233.

subject matter of Old Testament theology coequal with "the spiritual and religious world of Israel and the conditions of her soul in general, nor is it her world of faith, all of which can only be reconstructed by means of conclusions drawn from the documents ..."[66] Rather, and in probably the most rehearsed statement in von Rad's work, Old Testament theology has as its subject matter, "Israel's own explicit assertions about Jahweh."[67] This simple and straightforward account of the task proved to be much more complicated than presented. As Christopher Seitz states, "What appeared to be a simple point of departure ... turned out to involve matters of a historical nature, requiring a complex extraction from the literature of a point of view, 'Israel's,' to be ranged on a grid of evolving traditions."[68] Von Rad's particular form of historical criticism, namely tradition criticism, provided the means for coming to terms with what Israel's "explicit assertions" actually were in her history of salvation.

We can observe the multifronted war von Rad fought. Old Testament theology needs to follow closely Israel's own confessional posture regarding the identity and ways of God. This demands detailed attention to the biblical documents with this kerygmatic focus in mind. Israel's confessional life embedded in the Old Testament documents has something to say about her God; one must follow these documents rather than lead them with preconceived notions about a particular "center" (*Mitte*) of the Old Testament or an approach to the material that diverges from their intention as confessional literature. Especially important with this latter claim is keeping distinct historical-critical reconstructions of Israel's ancient history (etic) and Israel's own account of her history in spiritualized, poetic form (emic). "The fact that these two views of Israel's history are so divergent is one of the most serious burdens imposed today upon biblical scholarship."[69]

These divergent accounts of Israel's history do not weigh von Rad down, however. He is following Israel's own confessional account of her history and is comfortable with more empirically oriented, scientific approaches to Israel's history having their say. Again, one should not confuse Israel's

---

66. Gerhard von Rad, *Old Testament Theology*, trans. D. M. G. Stalker (New York: Harper, 1962), 1:105.

67. Ibid.

68. Christopher R. Seitz, *Word with End: The Old Testament as Abiding Theological Witness* (Grand Rapids: Eerdmans, 1998), 32.

69. Von Rad, *Old Testament Theology*, 1:108.

kerygmatic account of her history with the historian's critical retrieval of Israel's "real" history.

History plays a central role in von Rad's approach to Old Testament theology because it plays such a central role in the Old Testament's self-presentation. "This implies that in principle Israel's faith is grounded in a theology of history. It regards itself as based upon historical acts, and as shaped and reshaped by factors in which it saw the hand of Jahweh at work."[70] These historical acts of Yahweh whose roots can be traced back to Israel's earliest confessions continue to be received afresh in Israel's confessional life. "It was a message so living and actual for each moment that it accompanied her on her journey through time, interpreting itself afresh to every generation, and informing every generation what it had to do."[71]

Von Rad's Old Testament theology resisted a static approach that sought for a center to the Old Testament, like "covenant" was for Eichrodt. For von Rad, Israel's theology found in the Old Testament documents is more dynamic and alive, rooted in God's historical acts of salvation for his people that are received in Israel's traditions and refitted again and again in Israel's confessional life before God. Summarizing the matter well, von Rad concludes, "Thus, retelling remains the most legitimate form of theological discourse on the Old Testament."[72]

Conclusion

Von Rad's early tradition-historical work became the critical means by which he engaged the Old Testament's theology and, eventually, the typological relationship of the Old Testament to the New Testament as well. Brevard Childs summarizes von Rad's tradition-critical approach:

> In sum, von Rad's understanding of actualization provided him with a hermeneutical means of resolving a host of persistent problems respecting the Old Testament. First, he was able to assign theological value to each stage in the lengthy process of historical development by treating the multilayered text as a witness to Israel's struggle to contemporize the past. Secondly, the continuing process allowed him to retain the diversity of the Old Testament within a broad theological movement from prophecy to fulfillment. Finally, the text's openness to

---

70. Ibid., 1:106.
71. Ibid., 1:112.
72. Ibid., 1:121.

the future provided an avenue for Christians to find a dynamic analogy for subsequent appropriation of an ancient legacy.[73]

Von Rad's critical investigation of the Old Testament is much more far-reaching than this brief rehearsal states. He worked on the Prophets in volume two of his Old Testament theology. Toward the end of his career, he turned to the Wisdom Literature. Von Rad also had a continuing interest in the Christian reception of the Old Testament as a typological witness and even engaged in an interesting debate with Wilhelm Vischer concerning his approach to the Christian witness of the Old Testament, which von Rad vehemently rejected.[74] Ultimately, von Rad built his understanding of the relationship between the Old and New Testaments on the back of his historical-critical project; i.e., the New Testament was another layer of growth and reception of Israel's earlier traditions. Vischer seemed representative of another time with his "allegorical" approach.

But others challenge von Rad precisely at this juncture between him and Vischer. Jon Levenson, for example, finds von Rad's tradition-critical instincts deficient when it comes to Old Testament and biblical theology. For Levenson, von Rad's attempt to give an account of the New Testament's relationship to the Old Testament with methods inherited from historical criticism ultimately fails. The enterprise unravels because the New Testament's account of Jesus Christ and his relationship to the traditions of Israel do not fit tidily into a tradition-historical account. The constraining role that faith plays in ordering our knowledge and our approach to the material and formal matters of Christian canon come in too late for von Rad. In Levenson's terms, "He expected faith to stop Heraclitus's river."[75] Von Rad prioritized the forward-leaning motion of Israel's tradi-

---

73. Brevard S. Childs, "Gerhard von Rad in American Dress," in *The Hermeneutical Quest: Essays in Honor of James Luther Mays on His Sixty-Fifth Birthday*, ed. Donald G. Miller (Allison Park, Pa.: Pickwick, 1986), 79. Childs's larger point in this fine essay is to distance von Rad from a particular American tendency to deploy his understanding of actualization in a way foreign to von Rad himself. "Von Rad's concern with the traditioning process and his demand for flexible, dynamic interpretation relates directly to his Christological concern to do justice to the full dimension of God's revelation in Jesus Christ" (p. 83). The flexibility von Rad allows for is attached to his understanding of the finality of God's revelation in Jesus Christ.

74. On this matter, see Rendtorff, *Canon and Theology*, 76–92; Brevard Childs, "Does the Old Testament Witness to Jesus Christ," in *Evangelium Schriftauslegung Kirche: Festschrift für Peter Stuhlmacher zum 65. Geburtstag*, ed. Jostein Adna, Scott J. Hafemann, and Otfried Hofius (Göttingen: Vandenhoeck & Ruprecht, 1997), 57–64.

75. Jon D. Levenson, *The Hebrew Bible, the Old Testament, and Historical Criticism* (Louisville: Westminster John Knox, 1993), 24.

tions over the canonical text itself as a stable witness to God's identity and ways. The result was the loss of the anterior authority of the Old Testament witness as a canonically constraining voice for the New Testament. The Old Testament itself was only one stage in a linear, redemptive historical schema as it leaned into the New Testament. A Christian approach to biblical theology has traditionally allowed the New Testament to lean back into the Old Testament as well because of the shared subject matter of both Testaments.

FOR FURTHER READING

Childs, Brevard S. "Gerhard von Rad in American Dress." Pages 77 – 86 in *The Hermeneutical Quest: Essays in Honor of James Luther Mays on His Sixty-Fifth Birthday*, edited by Donald G. Miller. Allison Park, Pa.: Pickwick, 1986.

Crenshaw, James L. *Gerhard von Rad.* Waco, Tex.: Word, 1978.

Groves, Joseph W. *Actualization and Interpretation in the Old Testament.* Society of Biblical Literature Dissertation Series 86. Atlanta: Scholars Press, 1987.

Hayes, John H., and Frederick Prussner. *Old Testament Theology: Its History and Development.* Atlanta: John Knox Press, 1985.

Knight, Douglas A. *Rediscovering the Traditions of Israel*, 3rd ed. Studies in Biblical Literature. Atlanta: Society of Biblical Literature, 2006.

Levenson, Jon D. *The Hebrew Bible, the Old Testament, and Historical Criticism.* Louisville: Westminster John Knox, 1993.

Levinson, Bernard M. "Reading the Bible in Nazi Germany: Gerhard von Rad's Attempt to Reclaim the Old Testament for the Church." *Interpretation* 62 (2008): 238 – 54.

Oeming, Manfred. "Gerhard von Rad as a Theologian of the Church." *Interpretation* 62 (2008): 231 – 37.

Rendtorff, Rolf. *Canon and Theology: Overtures to an Old Testament Theology.* Translated by Margaret Kohl. Overtures to Biblical Theology. Minneapolis: Fortress, 1993.

———. *The Problem of the Process of Transmission in the Pentateuch.* Translated by John J. Scullion. Journal for the Study of the Old Testament: Supplement Series. Sheffield, JSOT, 1990.

continued on next page

Seitz, Christopher R. *Word with End: The Old Testament as Abiding Theological Witness*. Grand Rapids: Eerdmans, 1998.

Smend, Rudolf. *From Astruc to Zimmerli: Old Testament Scholarship in Three Centuries*. Translated by M. Kohl. Tübingen: Mohr Siebeck, 2007.

von Rad, Gerhard. "The Form-Critical Problem of the Hexateuch." Pages 1 – 58 in *From Genesis to Chronicles: Explorations in Old Testament Theology*. Translated by E. W. T. Dicken. Minneapolis: Fortress, 2005.

——. *Old Testament Theology*. 2 vols. Translated by D. M. G. Stalker. New York: Harper, 1962, 1965.

WILLIAM FOXWELL ALBRIGHT
(1891–1971)

Digging Deeply into Israel's History

THE PAST CENTURY WITNESSED AN EXPLOSION IN THE FIELD OF BIBLICAL archaeology. Great strides have been made in advancing our understanding of the culture, lives, and literature of ancient peoples — even Julius Wellhausen was not fully impacted by the burgeoning field of Assyriology in his day. Biblical archaeology is not a discipline that has remained locked in the academy. Much of the public imagination has been captured by the investigation of antiquities: What really happened in ancient Egypt, Israel, Greece, and Rome? Television documentaries, popular movies, and glossy magazines have sparked interest and created a sense of romance for the field. Though the actual practice of biblical archaeology is probably more marked by sweat, digging, and dusting than the lore attached to finding the lost ark of the covenant, the pursuit of ancient civilizations in physical artifacts is a venerated discipline in the academy and broader culture. If one name stands at the headwaters of this booming discipline, it is William Foxwell Albright.

The Dean of Biblical Archaeologists

Albright's destiny as the "dean of biblical archaeologists" was set at an early age.[1] He grew up in an educated family, the son of Methodist missionaries

---

1. Much of the biographical information on Albright is gleaned from Leona Glidden Running and David Noel Freedman, *William Foxwell Albright: A Twentieth-Century Genius* (New York: Morgan, 1975); see also Leona Glidden Running, "Albright, William Foxwell," in *Historical Handbook of Major Biblical Interpreters*, ed. Donald K. McKim (Downers Grove, Ill.: InterVarsity, 1998), 103–7.

in Chile. The oldest of six children, Albright's education was shaped by his mother and father and reinforced by tutoring his younger siblings. By the age of twelve, he was fluent in Spanish and learned in French and German. Life in Chile for an American boy was not a country picnic. Albright was teased and physically harassed by the "street urchins."[2] His mother and father even spanked him when he shied away from going into the Chilean streets on errands for them. As one can imagine, the environment of the Albright home was austere, strict, and single-minded, developing in him traits that were important for his life's vocation.

When Albright was ten years old (1901), his parents struck a deal with the young man. If he would walk to the bakery and deliver the bread to their home, thus saving them the money for delivery, they would give him the money in return (eventually Albright could no longer stomach this bread because he saw a live chicken in the bakery walking in the bread bin!).[3] There was no doubt in young Albright's mind where his money would go. A farming accident at his grandmother Foxwell's Iowa farm had crippled his left hand at the age of five.[4] Albright also suffered from myopia due to contracting typhoid fever as a child. These physical ailments made normal childhood activities difficult for him. When others played sports, Albright preferred books. When he had earned the necessary five dollars, he purchased R. W. Rogers's two-volume *The History of Babylonia and Assyria*. His parents withheld the books until Christmas (an understandable but unfortunate lapse in parental judgment). Once they were in his hands, Albright absorbed their contents. By the age of eleven, Albright knew he was going to be a biblical archaeologist. Leona Glidden Running observes that Albright's only fear was "that by time he grew up, everything would have been discovered."[5]

Mission work proved difficult on the family's health, especially William's father, Wilbur. After serving for thirteen years on the foreign field, the Albright family returned to Iowa. These teenage years were not happy for William. His father moved from one parsonage to another. The intellectual surroundings were less than stimulating.[6] When William turned fifteen, the family moved to Fayette, Iowa, near the farm of Grandmother

---

2. Running and Freedman, *William Foxwell Albright*, 1.
3. Ibid., 10.
4. Ibid., 103.
5. Ibid.
6. Ibid., 12.

Albright. This move to Fayette was the silver lining in young William's dark cloud.

Nestled in the town of Fayette was Upper Iowa University. Here, as a sixteen-year-old, Albright attended the "senior academy" preparatory school of the university.[7] During this period, he taught himself Hebrew from his father's copy of Harper's inductive textbook. While at UIU, Albright also studied Greek, Latin, Akkadian, and mathematics. He also enjoyed debating and literary clubs. He published his first article in 1911. It appeared in the *Upper Iowa Academician*, a periodical that presented the ideas of the "Genius Club," a club begun by Albright's religion professor at UIU. The subject of Albright's paper was "Recent Discoveries at Elephantine."[8] In time, Albright would recognize UIU as a culturally narrow institution. Nonetheless, he was grateful for an affordable education and the solid grounding he received in math and ancient languages.

After graduation, Albright had a one-year stint as a high school principal in South Dakota. It was a less-than-happy year for Albright that included a fistfight between one of his students and him.[9] As one might imagine, he did not have a taste for this level of education. During this exile year, Albright sought to realize his desires for further education. He was not hopeful about his applications for advanced study, a feeling that many who have applied for graduate studies will understand. But his insecurities were misplaced. Albright had written an article on the Akkadian word *dallalu* in the Gilgamesh Epic. He suggested the word meant "bat" (the flying kind) and cleared up a problem that had perplexed scholars. The article was accepted for publication in a leading German periodical, *Orientalistische Literaturzeitung.*[10] This was quite an achievement for the young Albright, which would eventually open the door for advanced studies.

Albright applied to study under Professor Paul Haupt at Johns Hopkins University. Haupt was a towering figure in his day. At the young age of twenty-one, he established the fact that Sumerian was a language.[11] He is remembered most for his *Polychrome Bible*, a color-coded edition that identified the J, E, D, and P sources. These examples only hint at the enormity of Haupt's contribution. J. M. Sasson summarizes, "Eventually,

---

7. Ibid., 13.
8. Ibid., 15.
9. Ibid., 21.
10. Ibid.
11. J. M. Sasson, "Albright as an Orientalist," *Biblical Archaeologist* 56 (1993): 4.

Haupt's bibliography of over 600 items had books and articles, some of them written in modern Hebrew, that spilled beyond Assyriology into Egyptology, Germanics, and the classics."[12] As a leading Orientalist in his day, he founded the Oriental Seminary at Johns Hopkins, which is today called the Department of Near Eastern Studies. Haupt read Albright's article and was impressed with his potential. He offered him a spot at Johns Hopkins University and a $500 fellowship. Awarding Albright the fellowship was significant because Haupt had never before awarded it to an unmatriculated student.[13]

Albright's future as a scholar was taking shape. His ambition was only outdone by his hard work. Remember, this was a young man who taught himself Hebrew and Akkadian, along with study of French, German, Latin, and Greek. His sister recalled an encounter the summer before William entered Johns Hopkins. "One evening when Mother and I were in the kitchen and it was about dark, William appeared at the door and in a very mysterious tone said, 'I am neither man nor woman; I am neither brute nor human — I'm a scholar!'"[14] Albright summed up his ambition: "I'm going to be a scholar and live in an attic!"[15]

William thrived at Johns Hopkins. The close study of Hebrew, Arabic, and cuneiform (this word comes from the Latin and means "wedge-shaped"; it refers to the triangle-shaped marks used in various northwest Semitic languages, e.g., Sumerian and Akkadian) gave his eyes considerable trouble, however. He would have to rest them, which frustrated his desire for rapid advancement in his studies. William also suffered from a broken engagement to his college sweetheart during this period; this was a particularly stressful moment. Determined to become a scholar, he pressed on despite these setbacks. He was awarded the Rayner Fellowship after his first year of study, a fellowship worth $50 more than his initial one. With great earnestness, Albright studied the languages of the ancient Near East, biblical criticism, geography, archaeology, history, and epigraphy. During this period, Albright distinguished himself as a promising scholar of the ancient world. He presented papers at professional meetings, published articles in *The Journal of the American Oriental Society*, and

---

12. Ibid., 4 – 5.
13. Running and Freedman, *William Foxwell Albright*, 24.
14. Ibid., 25 – 26.
15. Ibid., 26.

was appointed to Phi Beta Kappa by Professor Haupt. He also received the prestigious Thayer Fellowship from Yale University, which would eventually provide Albright a year's study in Palestine. Albright completed his dissertation on "The Assyrian Deluge Epic" and received his doctorate in June 1916. Albright was the scholar he had aimed to be.

Albright continued at Johns Hopkins for another two years after his doctorate. He taught courses and pursued his own studies in ancient languages and history. During this period, Professor Haupt revealed his desire for Albright to be his successor as chair of the Oriental Seminary. But Albright's failing health during this period made him reluctant to accept such a post; he was at the end of himself physically. To add insult to injury, Albright was drafted into military service in 1918, toward the end of World War I. Albright was so worn down when he arrived at Camp Syracuse in New York that he fainted during his physical examination.[16] These six months of service as a clerk and potato peeler proved difficult and important in William's life. He had time for free thought and critical reflection on the bewildering amount of data in his first-class mind. More than this, Albright had time to reflect on spiritual matters. Ever referring to God's providence in his life, Albright wrestled with his faith, higher-critical approaches to the Bible, and his frustration with the narrow dogmatism of his father. He found that the people surrounding him did not need the ideas of higher criticism. Albright wrote, "The men needed only the simple faith of the Nazarene, as everyone did."[17] Albright was struggling after the truth. He was also gaining physical strength and improving his health during this period. Though difficult, this season in the army was a good interruption in the young scholar's life.[18]

William spent the next decade of his life in Palestine. He took advantage of the Thayer Fellowship in 1919, spending the year at the American School of Oriental Research (ASOR). While in Palestine, he studied modern Hebrew and modern Arabic, as well as topography and archaeology. He took trips by foot, car, and horseback to various archaeological sites in Palestine. He also journeyed to Lebanon, Syria, Egypt, and Iraq.[19] In addition, he married Dr. Ruth Norton in 1921, a Hopkins PhD in Sanskrit. Ruth

---

16. Ibid., 48.
17. Ibid., 49–50.
18. Ibid., 52.
19. Gus W. Van Beek, "William Foxwell Albright: A Short Biography," in *The Scholarship of William Foxwell Albright: An Appraisal*, ed. Gus W. Van Beek (Atlanta: Scholars Press, 1989), 8.

had transferred to John Hopkins after meeting William at a professional meeting held at Yale. In this same year, Albright was named director of the Jerusalem school of the ASOR, and he remained there until 1929. These were fruitful and stimulating years in Albright's life. Three of his four sons were born in Jerusalem during his tenure as director of ASOR. His archaeological studies began with excavations at Tell el-Fûl ("mound, or hill, of the bean") in 1922 and 1923.[20] In 1926, he participated in an excavation at Tell Beit Mirsim. These excavations carried Albright into the 1930s, when he began work at Beth-Zur and revisited the sites mentioned above.[21] Excavating archaeological sites and cataloging the discoveries proved to be exhausting work. In fact, Ruth Albright's physician encouraged her to sleep in a separate room from William if she was to have any sleep. He would arrive home from the digs late at night. Then he would open mail and study in their bedroom late into the evening, causing sleep deprivation for both of them. Running and Freedman write, "Ruth had known that she was marrying a genius and that geniuses are not easy to live with, and she simply adjusted herself to their life the best she could, in a way to protect his genius and productivity in scholarly work."[22]

In 1929, William resigned as full-time director of ASOR. He took the W. W. Spence Chair in Semitic Languages at Johns Hopkins University, the chair held by Professor Haupt until his death in 1926. Albright maintained a close connection to the Jerusalem school. He became editor of the *Bulletin of the American Schools of Oriental Research* (*BASOR*) in 1930, a role he filled for the next thirty-eight years. In 1933, Albright again became director of the Jerusalem school, but on a half-year cooperation with John Hopkins, which allowed Albright to continue his archaeological work in Palestine.[23]

In the midst of his teaching and archaeological work, Albright maintained a rigorous research and writing life. In 1932, he published a series of lectures titled *The Archaeology of Palestine and the Bible*. His interest in philology continued as well. In 1934, he published *The Vocalization of the Egyptian Syllabic Orthography*. The book for which Albright is best known, *From the Stone Age to Christianity*, appeared in 1940. In this work,

---

20. Running and Freedman, *William Foxwell Albright*, 106.

21. For Albright's explanation of these sites and the process of choosing them, see William Foxwell Albright, *The Archaeology of Palestine* (Baltimore, Md.: Penguin, 1949), 7 – 8.

22. Running and Freedman, *William Foxwell Albright*, 107.

23. Van Beek, "William Foxwell Albright," 8 – 9.

Albright demonstrated by archaeological research and the comparative method (more on this below) the substantial historicity of the Bible. *From the Stone Age to Christianity* also presented a philosophy of history more akin to scientific research than the subjective and literary approaches of Wellhausen a generation before. This work also revealed that Albright's interest in archaeology was primarily related to his interest in the Bible.

Albright's next major publication was *Archaeology and the Religion of Palestine* (1942), a book based on lectures given at Colgate-Rochester Divinity School the previous year. Much of this book is a streamlined presentation of the main arguments in *From the Stone Age to Christianity*. In 1949, he published a popular-level book titled *The Archaeology of Palestine*, a book meant to provide a clear and accessible presentation of the method and findings of the biblical archaeological movement. Albright continued researching, writing, and lecturing. In time, more of his research appeared, such as *The Biblical Period from Abraham to Ezra* (1963), *The Proto-Sinaitic Inscriptions and Their Decipherment* (1966), and *Yahweh and the Gods of Canaan* (1968). Toward the end of his career, Albright devoted much time and labor to his role as coeditor with David Noel Freedman of the Anchor Bible series. This series, whose focus was a new translation of biblical books, textual/exegetical work, and new insights gained from the field of comparative methodology, is a standard in commentary literature to this day. Albright's breadth of interest and ability is demonstrated in his own work on *Matthew* in this series (which appeared posthumously). His publishing legacy amounts to more than one thousand publications and is the result of a lifetime of devotion to his discipline and students.

The list of honorary degrees, titles, and awards given to Albright is staggering.[24] Albright's own contribution to the field of biblical archaeology and the comparative method as seen above is beyond substantial. Still, one of Albright's greatest contributions to biblical scholarship is his numerous students who almost single-handedly took over the field of Old Testament scholarship in the United States. Gus Van Beek speculates that the number of Albright's students ranges from seventy-five to one hundred.[25] Many of these students are the dons of Old Testament scholarship and ancient Near Eastern Studies, including David Noel Freedman, Frank Cross, George Ernest Wright, John Bright, and George Mendenhall. John

---

24. Ibid., 12–13.
25. Ibid., 14.

Bright's *A History of Israel*, a compendium of Albright's views, is the best-known history of Israel to come out of the twentieth century.[26]

Albright's students had great respect and affection for their mentor. He was a demanding teacher but was equally caring toward his students. There are several stories of Albright offering personal financial aid to his "boys" in need.[27] An unusual paternal link existed between Albright and his students. Their desire for his approval had the marks of the honor and shame cultures of the ancient civilizations they studied.[28] Burke Long recounts, "A student of Frank Cross ... reported many years later that 'Cross revered Albright, and he even told us that he never published anything that disagreed with Albright until after Albright died, out of respect for Albright.'"[29] The affection of Albright's students is marked with irony. Albright confessed to Freedman and others that his biggest disappointment in life was his students. Freedman believed this was the case because Albright overestimated his students' abilities.[30]

In the 1950s, a colloquium, or "learned society," was established by George Ernest Wright. This biblical colloquium met in tandem with the Society of Biblical Literature and Exegesis and was composed of members who were either former students of Albright's or those sympathetic with his approach to the discipline; those associated within the trajectory of Albright's approach were called the "Baltimore school."[31] This was a private, by-invitation-only group, and Albright was indeed the founding father.[32] If an analogy can be made to popular culture, Albright was as much the godfather as founding father. Burke Long's less-than-flattering account of this institution portrays it as a powerful social mechanism whose goal was simple: to take over biblical studies in the United States.[33] Though this goal was never fully realized, the disciplines related to the comparative method in Old Testament studies have had a far-reaching influence on biblical scholarship across the theological spectrum, from

---

26. Burke O. Long, *Planting and Reaping Albright: Politics, Ideology, and Interpreting the Bible* (University Park, Pa.: Penn State Univ. Press, 1997), 57–59.

27. See chapter 12 of Running and Freedman, *William Foxwell Albright*.

28. Ibid.

29. Long, *Planting and Reaping Albright*, 18.

30. Running and Freedman, *William Foxwell Albright*, 210.

31. The Society of Biblical Literature and Exegesis was the earlier name of the Society of Biblical Literature.

32. Long, *Planting and Reaping Albright*, 15–16.

33. Ibid., 20–21. I have benefited greatly from Don Collett's unpublished paper, "Hermeneutics in Context: Comparative Method and Modern Evangelical Scholarship."

university religion departments to evangelical approaches to Old Testament studies and apologetics. Though Albright's assessment of the archaeological data has been challenged, his influence as the dean of biblical archaeologists is present to this day. He died on September 19, 1971 in Baltimore, Maryland.

A life as full and round as Albright's is deserving of much more than this modest account. As the standard biography on him expresses in its title, he was a twentieth-century genius. Nevertheless, our attention turns now to Albright's method — the comparative method. How exactly did Albright approach the study of the Old Testament in light of the historical data being uncovered from the burgeoning discipline of archaeology?

Albright, the Comparative Method, and Historical Positivism

During the 1940s and 1950s, there were two great schools of Old Testament critical investigation — the Alt-Noth school (named after Albrecht Alt and Martin Noth) and the Albright school. Both of these schools were invested in the question of Israel's history. At the same time, their approach to the subject differed in method. The Alt-Noth school approached Israel's history primarily by the means of critical analysis of the biblical text. Albright's school sought to confirm the historicity of the biblical text by beginning with an external norm — archaeology and the ancient Near Eastern contextual situation of Israel's history. Literary-critical matters played a lesser role for Albright than historical correlation of biblical claims and archaeological data.

Alt still believed in the enduring legacy of Julius Wellhausen's understanding of Israel's religious-historical development. When Albright wrote to Alt commending him on the publication of his *The Source of Israelite Law*, Alt responded tartly, "But Wellhausen remains Wellhausen!"[34] The Alt-Noth school's approach to Israel's history assumed the disjointed character between the biblical narratives and the historical events reported therein. For example, Alt proposed in his *The Settlement of the Israelites in Palestine* that Israel's possession of the land of Canaan was really a progressive and peaceful venture of seminomadic tribes settling into an agricultural way of life. The movement into the land happened over a long period as the search for better grazing land turned into a settled way of

---

34. Quoted in Rudolf Smend, *From Astruc to Zimmerli: Old Testament Scholarship in Three Centuries*, trans. M. Kohl (Tübingen: Mohr Siebeck, 2007), 151.

life.[35] Alt's historical description differed markedly from the biblical portrayal of the conquest of the land. Albright reacted strongly against this understanding of the settlement of the land.

The Alt-Noth school's approach, like Gerhard von Rad's approach to Old Testament theology, separated the faith of Israel from the historicity of the events described in their literary heritage. In other words, the faith of Israel witnessed to in the Old Testament did not depend on the historical veracity of the events portrayed. According to Alt, the Bible does not give us history. (This was an instinct observed in de Wette over a century before.) It gives us Israel's faith-based understanding of her history, which is quite different from Israel's actual history. For Albright, the *essential* historical character of the Old Testament narratives was integral to the authority of the Bible, even if the reporting of the events in the Old Testament was blurry in the details.[36]

Though the Albright and Alt-Noth schools did differ in approach, there is more overlap in intentions and goals than first meets the eye. Both schools believed that the biblical portrayal of Israel's history was not "an entirely accurate account."[37] Both schools were interested in questions that lay behind the material form of the text as it stands in its canonical form. For Alt-Noth, the question of Israel's religious traditions, their original *Sitz im Leben*, and the dynamic reception of those traditions in Israel's literary documents provided the focus of the historical approach. Albright focused on correlating the biblical history to an external norm that lay behind the text as well, namely, the archaeological evidence and the religious cultures of the ancient Near East. J. Maxwell Miller clarifies:

> Both the Altians and the Albrightians recognized that the biblical presentation of Israel's history is not entirely accurate as it stands; both were confident nevertheless that historically useful data could be derived from the biblical materials; and both insisted that the nonbiblical sources should be granted an integrity of their own rather than simply harmonized or explained away in deference to the biblical account.[38]

---

35. Douglas A. Knight, *Rediscovering the Traditions of Israel*, 3rd ed. (Studies in Biblical Literature; Atlanta: Society of Biblical Literature, 2006), 73.

36. The labels *essential* and *detailed* are borrowed from the important essay by J. Maxwell Miller ("Israelite History," in *The Hebrew Bible and Its Modern Interpreters*, ed. Gene M. Knight and Douglas A. Knight [Chico, Calif.: Scholars Press, 1985], 20).

37. Ibid., 21.

38. Ibid.

Though the two schools differed in approach and in level of confidence attached to the correlation of the Bible to the empirical history of Israel — in today's terminology, Alt-Noth were minimalist, and Albright a maximalist — at the end of the day, both approaches sought to establish the veracity of something that lay behind the actual text itself.[39] As Albright said of biblical archaeology in one of his later publications, "Increasingly we shall be able to reconstruct successive cultures, to date them within very narrow limits, and to confirm, illustrate, and correct in detail the biblical historical tradition."[40]

In an important article describing Albright's view of biblical archaeology, Frank Cross locates Albright's project within the history of religions.[41] As observed previously with Hermann Gunkel (most specifically in his earlier work), the history of religions school approached the Old Testament with "Herder's passion" for locating the Old Testament in the context of its surrounding cultural and religious milieu.[42] This religious-historical (*Religionsgeschichte*) approach to Old Testament studies is also called the "comparative method" because comparisons are drawn between Israel's religious faith and the Canaanite and ancient Near Eastern world. Albright was indefatigable in his search for parallels between Israel's culture and the culture of the Near East, even though, in time, he saw the problems of such an approach.[43]

As is recalled, Gunkel's religious-historical approach turned more heavily toward the analysis of Israel's literary traditions by means of form-critical analysis. The literary unit was detached from its surrounding canonical context for the sake of providing a two-way interpretive street between the identified literary unit and the original *Sitz im Leben* out of which the material grew. The literary unit provided a window onto the

---

39. Rolf Rendtorff (*Canon and Theology: Overtures to an Old Testament Theology*, ed. Margaret Kohl [Overtures to Biblical Theology; Minneapolis: Fortress, 1993], 26) confirms this conclusion:

At first glance, the intention of the Alt school was entirely different or even contradictory. Their main concern was with the texts themselves. But they, too, had the intention of finding something behind the texts, in this case, the *traditions* which found expression in the texts. They also tried to reconstruct history, namely the history of traditions, their origins, their *Sitz in Leben* in certain institutions, mainly cultic ones, and the way these traditions reached written form. One could say these scholars were interested in the prehistory of the texts.

40. William F. Albright, *New Horizons in Biblical Research* (London: Oxford Univ. Press, 1966), 4.

41. Frank M. Cross, "W. F. Albright's View of Biblical Archaeology and Its Methodology," *Biblical Archaeologist* 36 (1973): 2 – 5.

42. Ibid., 4.

43. Ibid.

original situation in life, and the original situation in life provided a herme-neutical grid for interpreting the unit. Albright was resistant to this kind of form-critical analysis because, at the end of the day, it was too subjec-tive and flimsy an approach. Cross writes, "He was wary of all syntheses constructed on the basis of internal biblical data alone."[44] Gunkel's form criticism and von Rad's tradition-critical approach lacked the firm grasp on the ancient material Albright sought to establish. These approaches were too dependent on the literary forms internal to the Bible itself and not concerned enough with establishing points of contact with Israel's empirical history outside its textual boundaries. Textually based theories of Israel's history would not provide the scientific precision that Albright was after. "One manuscript, one papyrus, he regarded as worth a thousand theories."[45]

Cross describes Albright as one of the last general Orientalists or bibli-cal archaeologists. Efforts have been made to change the name "biblical archaeology" to "Syro-Palestinian archaeology" (e.g., as can be seen in the work of William Dever). But Cross finds this problematic as it pertains to Albright because his interests were too broad for such a provincial descrip-tion. Albright's approach to the discipline was all-encompassing. Albright was a leading specialist in a particular field of archaeology — scientific ceramic typology. He was, in fact, the father of scientific ceramic typology. In this discipline, various kinds of vessels in a given region of the Levant are examined and classified.[46] How was the pot shaped at the rim? How was the handle crafted? What does the base of the pot look like? How is the pot finished and decorated?[47] A pottery chronology of Palestine was the result of Albright's detailed classification or typology as pots were assigned to a particular time in history. This provided an enormous aid for archae-ologists seeking to determine the particular date of a site discovered dur-ing a dig. For example, the inverted rim in clay pots helped to distinguish Bronze Age from Iron Age pots. In fact, ceramic typology is Albright's greatest contribution to biblical archaeology.[48]

Albright's specialized abilities were impressive and a great aid to bibli-cal archaeologists. At the same time, Albright lamented the specializa-

---

44. Ibid.

45. Ibid.

46. Peoples and cultures in the Near East around the Mediterranean Sea — from Turkey to Egypt.

47. Gus W. Van Beek, "W. F. Albright's Contribution to Archaeology," in *The Scholarship of William Foxwell Albright*, 66.

48. Ibid., 66 – 67. Albright discusses ceramic typology in his *The Archaeology of Palestine*, 116 – 18.

tion of archaeologists who were unable to bring together all the necessary components of a good archaeologist — critical understanding of the Bible, knowledge of Semitic languages, and historical studies (areas in which Albright himself was more than capable). Cross explains, "Biblical archaeology could never narrow to 'dirt archaeology.'"[49] And in this sense, Albright was a generalist. He had specialized knowledge across the entire field, with a broad range of historical and archaeological interests. "Biblical archaeology [for Albright] included papyri from Egypt, the onomasticon of the Amorites, a cylinder seal from Greece, Phoenician ivories from Spain, an ostracon from Edom, a painted Athenian pot, a skull from Carmel. In short, the whole ancient world, its literature, history, material culture belonged to the subject matter of biblical archaeology."[50] Few, if any, have been as adept at all these fields as Albright. He was a "master typologist" who produced rigorous methods for identifying the historical development of ancient civilizations by the study of their artifacts — ceramic types, linguistic change, proper names (onomastics), and ancient writing (paleography).[51]

Moreover, for Albright, a pot or a papyrus is worth more than a thousand theories because one can touch and classify a pot. One can apply rigorous and assured scientific methods to these various typologies, unlike literary-critical theories developed by figures such as Wellhausen. The confidence Albright attached to archaeology's role in establishing the veracity of the Bible is remarkable in retrospect. The concluding postscript of his *Archaeology and the Religion of Israel* makes this claim:

> Since the Old Testament is historical in essence as well as in canonical purpose, archaeology becomes an indispensable aid to our understanding of it. *Only through archaeological research can biblical history become a scientific discipline*, since history can in general become scientific only by the consistent application of archaeological or other equally rigorous methodology.[52]

Albright's statement regarding history as a scientific discipline shares features in common with what is called "historical positivism" or "logical

---

49. Cross, "W. F. Albright's View of Biblical Archaeology," 3.

50. Ibid.

51. Ibid, 4.

52. William Foxwell Albright, *Archaeology and the Religion of Israel* (Baltimore, Md.: Johns Hopkins Press, 1953), 176, emphasis mine; see also William Foxwell Albright, *From the Stone Age to Christianity: Monotheism and the Historical Process* (Baltimore, Md.: Johns Hopkins Press, 1946), 75–87.

positivism." Auguste Comte's vision in the 1830s of producing an historical method devoid of theological or metaphysical speculation and based on the senses alone has had a long shelf life. Comte's approach was wed to an empirical assessment of observable data in which speculation and imagination were subordinate to observation.[53] For Comte, the human mind has evolved along an identifiable linear pattern from the theological era (fetishism, polytheism, monotheism), to the metaphysical era (the human mind still incoherent), to the positive era (the human mind achieves coherence by rejecting absolutes and essences and seeks to understand the laws that govern relationships between various realities).[54] Albright rejected Comte's particular evolutionary theory of the human mind — fetishism, polytheism, and monotheism. This simple linear movement did not do justice to the complexities of religious phenomena in history.[55] He also had misgivings about a historical positivism that continually attempted to arrive at historical conclusions on the basis of the evidence alone — this is observed in Leopold von Ranke's (1795–1886) oft-repeated statement about history (*wie es eigentlich gewesen* [as it really happened]) — without providing a rubric by which to understand the data.[56]

Still, Albright's approach to history was built on analogy to the sciences. He dismissed contemporary thinkers who had made a sharp distinction between the sciences and historical investigation. Biography is necessarily an art and not an historical discipline because the judging of inner motives, even within a certain environment and education, is an impossible task. So the biographer hopes for a proximate accuracy but not a scientific one.[57] But with civilizations and historical movements the situation is more stable. Albright observes, "Archaeology and the history of civilization have proved that the material, social, and mental characteristics of a given culture are relatively stable and can generally be fixed with a decreasing margin of error as social organization becomes more primitive and less self-conscious or sophisticated."[58] The differences therefore

53. See Robert Audi, ed., *The Cambridge Dictionary of Philosophy*, 2nd ed. (Cambridge: Cambridge Univ. Press, 1999), 168–69.

54. See Ernst Breisach, *Historiography: Ancient, Medieval, and Modern* (Chicago: Univ. of Chicago Press, 2007), 272–73.

55. Albright, *From the Stone Age to Christianity*, 125.

56. Ibid., 48–50. Breisach (*Historiography*, 232–34) warns against too simplistic a reading of von Ranke's approach that does not take into account the universality of his vision.

57. Albright, *From the Stone Age to Christianity*, 78.

58. Ibid.

between the methods of science and history are relative and overlap in "logical method."[59]

In this sense, Albright's approach to history corresponds in significant ways to the neo-positivists of the 1920s and 1930s — Comte's initial vision restored without his less-than-favorable sociological accoutrements.[60] The argument is not being made here for a direct genetic link between the neo-positivists and Albright. Rather, the instincts are similar in that Albright, much like the neo-positivists, emphasized empirical and verifiable data over metaphysical speculation — as the reader recalls, a pot or a papyrus is more valuable than a thousand literary-critical theories. Albright's archaeological approach provided a reliable and external method by which the truth of the biblical claims could be judged according to the facts of history.[61] Speculation is set to the side, and assured results are brought to the center. In short, it is not a caricature to identify Albright's approach as historically positivist.

The philosophical underpinnings of Albright's historical approach have come undone. Reflecting on Albright's archaeological method, William Dever has this assessment:

> The assumption that archaeology is somehow more objective because it deals with things rather than ideas, that here the role of interpretation is less crucial than in the analysis of texts, and particularly the implication that archaeological data where available takes precedence over literary evidence — methodologically all this now seems incongruous.[62]

This assessment is affirmed when one observes the various interpretations of the archaeological data present today — e.g., Dever's denial of early Israel's monotheism (a position of extreme importance for Albright);

---

59. Ibid.

60. For more details, see Andrew Bowie, *Introduction to German Philosophy: From Kant to Habermas* (Cambridge, UK: Polity, 2003), 166 – 80; Breisach, *Historiography*, 378 – 80.

61. See Long, *Planting and Reaping Albright*, 138 – 41.

62. William Dever, "Syro-Palestinian and Biblical Archaeology," in *The Hebrew Bible and Its Modern Interpreters*, ed. Douglas A. Knight and Gene M. Tucker (Chico, Calif.: Scholars Press, 1985), 58 — though several pages later (p. 65), Dever makes this claim: "In short, archaeology — in the broad sense of the deliberate or chance recovery of ancient remains, including epigraphic evidence — is obviously our *only* possible source of new factual data capable of elucidating the Bible, without which we are reduced to the endless manipulation of the received texts or the application of ingenious but frequently inconclusive hypothesis. In that sense Albright's confidence in the external evidence provided by archaeology was not misplaced, merely premature."

differing accounts of the conquest of the land; or the denial of the existence of the Davidic monarchy by the Copenhagen school (so named because two of its main proponents teach at the University of Copenhagen; theirs is a minimalist approach to Israel's history, pushing much of the Old Testament literature late into the Persian period).[63] All of these conclusions lean on the archaeological "evidence."[64] As has become increasingly the case, the archaeological evidence is not as self-evident as Albright and some of his heirs tended to make out.[65]

It does not come as a surprise then to learn that David Noel Freedman, one of Albright's best-known students, describes the Oriental Seminary at Johns Hopkins as a place with a "strong Christian cultural bias, and an essentially apologetic approach to the subject of religion, especially biblical religion in (or against) its environment ..."[66] Freedman begins his reflection on Albright with, "Albright was not an historian."[67] At first glance, this seems like an audacious claim. But put in the context of the preceding comments, it is not. Freedman states that Albright was never really interested in writing a pan-history of the ancient Near East. As we have seen, Albright was certainly capable of such a task. But Albright's concern was not history per se but the Bible. Freedman says that his twin foci were the Bible on the one hand and comparative religion on the other.[68] Even a cursory glance at the titles of Albright's books reveals this commitment (e.g., *Archaeology and the Religion of Israel*; *From the Stone Age to Christianity*).

Albright occupied a middle ground between radical revisionists and biblical fundamentalists. He rejected the revisionists because they eviscerated the historical character of Scripture for something existential or lacking in substance (e.g., Bultmann's demythologizing project). At the same time, he rejected fundamentalists or ultraconservatives because they subordinated history to their own dogmatic claims. To claim the historical veracity of the Bible because "the Bible says so" lacks the intellectual

---

63. See Niels Peter Lemche, *The Old Testament Between Theology and History* (Louisville: Westminster John Knox, 2008).

64. William G. Dever, *Did God Have a Wife? Archaeology and Folk Religion in Ancient Israel* (Grand Rapids: Eerdmans, 2005), 252 – 303; Lemche, *Old Testament Between Theology and History*, 393 – 453.

65. It should be pointed out that Albright was ever willing to change his mind whenever the evidence demanded such a change.

66. David Noel Freedman, "W. F. Albright as an Historian," in *The Scholarship of William Foxwell Albright*, ed. Gus W. Van Beek, 35.

67. Ibid., 33.

68. Ibid., 34.

respectability Albright demanded.[69] As Freedman reports, "Albright could not forgive either party for obstructing the scientific search for truth."[70] The verifiable data Albright sought in the sands of the ancient Near Eastern desert did not live up to his optimism. Freedman says it forthrightly:

> After all the digging done and being done, how much has been accomplished?... Archaeology has not proved decisive or even greatly helpful in answering the questions most often asked by biblical scholars, and has failed to prove the historicity of persons and events especially at the early end of the scale.[71]

Freedman is not discounting the historical character of the Old Testament. He affirms its importance. But archaeology will only "illuminate and illustrate."[72] It will not substantiate the persons and events of the biblical material.[73] In short, archaeology is no substitute for faith.[74]

Care must be taken not to make light of the great achievement of archaeological discoveries in the late nineteenth and twentieth centuries, especially in the realm of comparative philology. The discovery of Akkadian and Ugaritic texts has been a great aid in situating biblical Hebrew in its Semitic context as a language that has features and vocabulary common to this family of languages.[75] The discovery of the Dead Sea Scrolls in

---

69. Ibid., 38.

70. Ibid.

71. Ibid., 39.

72. Ibid., 40.

73. "What texts could potentially make claims about the past similar to the Bible's claims? Outside the corpus of biblical literature, written sources from Iron Age Palestine are limited to scattered epigraphic remains. While these may provide small slices of information about Israel's past, they cannot substantiate the many historical scenarios in the Bible. On the other hand, records of military activity and imperial administration from the Egyptians, Assyrians, Babylonian, Persian, and Greek empires can potentially cohere with the Bible in places. For instance, the Assyrian invasion of Palestine in 701 BCE and the failure to capture Jerusalem is reported in the Bible and Assyrian annals, though naturally with differing slants. Rarely, however, are ancient Near Eastern sources and the Bible identifiably talking about the same event, as events important in one type of source usually do not show up in the other ... Consequently, the result of the search for extrabiblical texts for the history of ancient Israel have very few potential nonbiblical texts to start with, and even fewer whose claims can be directly correlated with a story in the Bible" (Megan Bishop Moore, *Philosophy and Practice in Writing a History of Ancient Israel* [Library of Hebrew Bible/Old Testament Studies; New York: T&T Clark, 2006], 147–48).

74. On the interplay of faith and belief in critical history, see especially C. Stephen Evans, *The Historical Christ and the Jesus of Faith: The Incarnational Narrative as History* (Oxford: Oxford Univ. Press, 1996), chapters 8 and 9.

75. See Christopher A. Rollston, *Writing and Literacy in the World of Ancient Israel: Epigraphic Evidence from the Iron Age* (Archaeology and Biblical Studies 11; Atlanta: Society of Biblical Literature, 2010).

1948 has undoubtedly changed the face of Old Testament studies. These documents have helped scholars understand the textual history of the Old Testament, its early textual reception, and scribal practices.[76] Background material and surrounding contextual matters in the ancient Near East have helped to situate Israel's religion amid its neighbors: with differences in comparative approaches ranging from total assimilation to the surrounding religions to the complete uniqueness of Israel's religion in the face of her neighbors.[77]

At the same time, a tension remains for those who resist a docetic account of the Old Testament that neuters its historical character and at the same time who recognize it as a living Word whose chief authorizing agent is God the Father, who has spoken in Jesus Christ by the Spirit. This tension creates difficulties for readers unwilling to dismiss the governing role that revelation plays in our account of Scripture's nature and our approach to reading it. Pertinent questions remain: What role does background material play in our reading of the Old Testament? When does background material become foreground material to such an extent that the biblical narratives, in Hans Frei's terminology, are eclipsed? Or when do Bible backgrounds, which again are helpful when used as *background*, become a Gnostic key for interpreters that unlocks the Bible in ways foreign to the interpretive instincts of the church? These are difficult questions that demand a theological account in light of our confession about the character of the Old Testament as Scripture. The Bible from Genesis to the maps, so to speak, is time conditioned and culturally situated. Certain matters demand to be engaged simply because of this reality (e.g., the fact that the Old Testament was written in Hebrew/Aramaic). But is a reconstruction of the world out of which the Bible arose, a world the reader should know is not carefully explicated in the biblical narratives themselves, the hermeneutical key that unlocks the strangeness of the Bible we encounter? Is the Bible's "problem" its historical distance? To repeat, these are important and difficult questions as readers of the Old Testament wrestle with its continuing role in the life of the church.

---

76. See Emanuel Tov, *Textual Criticism of the Hebrew Bible*, 3rd ed. (Minneapolis: Fortress, 2011).

77. As is seen in James Pritchard's *Ancient Near Eastern Texts* and the newer three-volume *The Context of Scripture*. A helpful guide through the morass of evidence is Kenton L. Sparks, *Ancient Texts for the Study of the Hebrew Bible: A Guide to the Background Literature* (Peabody, Mass.: Hendrickson, 2005). See also Benjamin D. Sommer's interesting work, *The Bodies of God and the World of Ancient Israel* (Cambridge: Cambridge Univ. Press, 2009).

Conclusion

William Foxwell Albright's vision for situating the Bible in its ancient Near Eastern setting spawned generations of scholars who have followed suit.[78] The biblical theology movement of the post-World War II era has its roots in the vision of Albright's comparative method of reading the Old Testament. Several of Albright's students were major forces in this movement. For example, George Ernest Wright's "mighty acts of God" approach to biblical theology locates these acts on a redemptive-historical timeline that leaned on the critical reconstruction of Israel's history in its cultural context. The biblical theology movement and the comparative method fed off one another as scholars wrestled to secure the theological character of the Old Testament's enduring witness. On this account, the theological character of the Old Testament rested in the events themselves, even as these events were detached from the literary forms in which they had been received. The Bible itself was not the locus of revelation, but the events *in se* were.

The irony of the biblical theology movement, as Langdon Gilkey so forcefully showed, was that for all the talk of the mighty acts of God in history, the movement was slow to identify the acts of God with real events occurring in time and space.[79] Gary Dorrien writes, "The differences between modern biblical theology and *biblical* theology were enormous."[80] For the biblical theology movement, these events revealed the ancient faith of Israel, which was itself a historical reality grounded in the ancient Near Eastern world. But as Gilkey shows, the Bible itself does not present the events in this metaphorical fashion. The Bible presents God as "an intervening, partisan, miracle-making divine agent."[81] The God of the

---

78. See Long, *Planting and Reaping Albright*; Dever, "Syro-Palestinian and Biblical Archaeology." The obvious point should be stressed that interest in ancient Near Eastern studies did not begin with Albright. There was a generation or two before him that rode the wave of rising interest, e.g., in Assyriology and Egyptology (see Peter Machinist, "The Road Not Taken: Wellhausen and Assyriology," in *Homeland and Exile: Biblical and Ancient Near Eastern Studies in Honor of Bustenay Oded*, ed. Gershon Galil, Mark Geller, and Alan Millard [Leiden: Brill, 2009], 469–531).

79. Langdon B. Gilkey, "Cosmology, Ontology, and the Travail of Biblical Language," *Journal of Religion* 41 (1961): 194–205.

80. Gary Dorrien, *The Making of American Liberal Theology: Crisis, Irony, and Postmodernity 1950–2005* (Louisville: Westminster John Knox, 2006), 276.

81. Ibid., 278. James Barr's *The Semantics of Biblical Language* (1961) did much to aid the death of the biblical theology movement. Barr exposed the faulty linguistic approach to semantics that supported the biblical theology movement's notion of the superiority of the Hebrew mind. The combined critiques of Gilkey and Barr were too much for the movement to overcome. See especially Brevard Childs, *Biblical Theology in Crisis* (Philadelphia: Westminster, 1970).

biblical theology movement was tamer and more modern than the God of the Bible.

Once the assured results of Albright's archaeological discoveries came undone with panoply of competing interpretations of the data, the confidence attached to Albright's scientific method faded.[82] Where Albright may have collapsed evidence and interpretation onto each other, their necessary distinction is much clearer today.[83] Many difficulties still remain for scholars who wish to do justice to the literary character of Scripture, its historical particularity, and how they relate. Despite the enduring and incredible character of his scholarly achievement, Albright's appeal to scientific methodology and assured results creates obstacles difficult to overcome.

FOR FURTHER READING

Albright, William Foxwell. *Archaeology and the Religion of Israel.* Baltimore, Md.: Johns Hopkins Press, 1953.

——. *The Archaeology of Palestine.* Baltimore: Penguin, 1949.

——. *From the Stone Age to Christianity: Monotheism and the Historical Process.* Baltimore, Md.: Johns Hopkins Press, 1946.

Cross, Frank M. "W. F. Albright's View of Biblical Archaeology and Its Methodology." *Biblical Archaeologist* 36 (1973): 2 – 5.

Dever, William G. *Did God Have a Wife? Archaeology and Folk Religion in Ancient Israel.* Grand Rapids: Eerdmans, 2005.

——. "Syro-Palestinian and Biblical Archaeology." Pages 31 – 74 in *The Hebrew Bible and Its Modern Interpreters.* Edited by Douglas A. Knight and Gene M. Tucker. Chico, Calif.: Scholars Press, 1985.

Freedman, David Noel, ed. *The Published Works of William Foxwell Albright: A Comprehensive Bibliography.* Cambridge, Mass: ASOR, 1975.

Freedman, David Noel. "W. F. Albright as an Historian." Pages 33 – 43 in *The Scholarship of William Foxwell Albright: An Appraisal.* Edited by Gus W. Van Beek. Atlanta: Scholars Press, 1989.

82. See Megan Bishop Moore's helpful account, *Philosophy and Practice in Writing a History of Ancient Israel.*
83. Ibid., 143 – 44.

Long, Burke O. *Planting and Reaping Albright: Politics, Ideology, and Interpreting the Bible*. University Park, Pa.: Penn State Univ. Press, 1997.

Miller, J. Maxwell. "Israelite History." Pages 1–30 in *The Hebrew Bible and Its Modern Interpreters*. Edited by Gene M. Knight and Douglas A. Knight. Chico, Calif.: Scholars Press, 1985.

Moore, Megan Bishop. *Philosophy and Practice in Writing a History of Ancient Israel*. Library of Hebrew Bible/Old Testament Studies. New York: T&T Clark, 2006.

Running, Leona Glidden, and David Noel Freedman. *William Foxwell Albright: A Twentieth-Century Genius*. New York: Morgan, 1975.

Sasson, J. M. "Albright as an Orientalist." *Biblical Archaeologist* 56 (1993): 3–7.

Sparks, Kenton L. *Ancient Texts for the Study of the Hebrew Bible: A Guide to the Background Literature*. Peabody, Mass.: Hendrickson, 2005.

Van Beek, Gus W. "W. F. Albright's Contribution to Archaeology." Pages 61–73 in *The Scholarship of William Foxwell Albright: An Appraisal*. Edited by Gus W. Van Beek. Atlanta: Scholars Press, 1989.

———. "William Foxwell Albright: A Short Biography." Pages 7–15 in *The Scholarship of William Foxwell Albright: An Appraisal*. Edited by Gus W. Van Beek. Atlanta: Scholars Press, 1989.

7

BREVARD S. CHILDS

(1923–2007)

Confessional and Critical

THE TERM *PARADIGM SHIFT* LINES THE FENCE BETWEEN OVERUSE AND cliché. Because of these dual dangers, a risk is run whenever the term is deployed to describe someone's thought. Ideas are at times labeled such when in fact they are important twists and turns in the field, but not necessarily paradigm shifts. With these dangers in mind, I will run the risk of describing Brevard Childs's canonical approach to Old Testament studies as indeed a paradigm shift. Or to put it more mildly, I will make use of Thomas Kuhn's understanding of paradigm shift to illustrate what occurred with respect to Childs's canonical approach to Old Testament studies.

Kuhn gives us the language to describe what happens when established paradigms in the sciences are challenged, leading to new and unprecedented ways of understanding the subject matter. Scientists tend to describe the advancement of their work with categories derived from their empirical viewpoint. On such an account, scientific theories are developed in a straightforward process of correction and refinement as theories are tested, corrected, and verified on the basis of observation. Kuhn's work demonstrates that such a smooth and linear account of scientific change rarely corresponds to what really happens when revolutions take place in the scientific world.

Scientific revolutions occur when the established paradigms do not provide answers to the anomalies that continue to pester scientists. New theories arrive on the scene and replace older theories. The newer theories appear almost apocalyptically, breaking in and displacing older ways of conceiving the problem. When this occurs, new ways of understanding the subject matter are opened to the scientist; a revolution has occurred that replaces the standard paradigms of normal science.[1] For example, if time and space are relative to each other, as Einstein demonstrated, then older ways of understanding the physical universe are displaced in an effort to understand the universe in light of this new paradigm of understanding.[2]

An analogy can be made from the sciences to biblical criticism in the modern period. The standard paradigm tended to move away from the biblical text in a backward direction of some sort. This is present in historicist approaches like Albright's that move from the text itself to establish the historical background out of which the text arose. The backward direction is evident in biblical criticism of the more literary stripe as well, whether in its source, form, tradition-historical, or redaction-critical vein. Source criticism seeks to divide the text into its original literary strata — J, E, D, and P, for example. By atomizing the text to its smallest units, form criticism moved from text to the original religious situation out of which the text arose in an effort to recreate the religious experience and ritual of ancient Israel. Tradition history engages the levels of tradition embedded within the text so as to appreciate the text's "depth dimension" in its own right: What was the theology of J? And according to the subject of this chapter, Brevard Childs notes, "Redaction criticism does not involve a new methodology, rather it seeks to reassert aspects of an earlier literary criticism which were overshadowed by the enthusiasm for [Hermann] Gunkel's programme."[3]

On these accounts, even when literary matters such as genre and poetics are given their due in the text itself, the final form and shaping of the material is a historical accident that has to be overcome in order to appreciate properly the religious, historical, or literary levels present in the complex amalgamation of the final form. On none of these standard accounts

---

1. For Kuhn's overview of the move from established paradigms in normal science to paradigm shifts resulting in scientific revolutions, see the introduction in Thomas S. Kuhn, *The Structure of Scientific Revolutions* (Chicago: Univ. of Chicago Press, 1996).

2. For a critical engagement of Kuhn's work, see Richard Rorty, *Philosophy and the Mirror of Nature* (Princeton, N.J.: Princeton Univ. Press, 1979), 322 – 56.

3. Brevard S. Childs, *Introduction to the Old Testament as Scripture* (Philadelphia: Fortress, 1979), 39.

is the final form of the text privileged in any sense. In fact, the final form is either an impediment to be overcome (source criticism) or the final editorial stage in a tradition-building process that is not privileged over earlier stages of development. Thus the presentation of the Pentateuch in its final form is not inherently more valuable than the theology of the Yahwist embedded in this final form, as in von Rad, for example. Biblical criticism tended to treat Old Testament texts in their final form as a stopping point on the way to a more inviting destination.

Childs's approach to Old Testament interpretation is a paradigm shift precisely because his approach moves toward the Old Testament's canonical form in the way in which Jews and Christians have received it, without completely dispensing with the achievements of biblical criticism in the modern period. Modern biblical criticism, to borrow John Barton's formulation, "brackets out" theological commitments on the front end of the reading process for the sake of objectivity.[4] One recalls Baruch Spinoza's displacement of confession in favor of the natural light of reason. Childs's canonical approach "brackets in" theological commitments, as the title of his groundbreaking work indicates — *Introduction to the Old Testament as Scripture*. As mentioned above, this does not mean that Childs dismisses modern biblical criticism. As we will see, his approach is modern and not an atavistic retrieval of a sunnier premodern day. Childs's canonical approach is a paradigm shift because, unlike any of his predecessors, it brings together a confessional *and* critical posture toward Old Testament interpretation, thus providing new avenues of insight and inquiry into the complexity of its canonical form. Where canon tends to be treated as a historical category tacked on to the end of Old Testament introduction, a part of the text's reception but not its compositional history, Childs brings canon to the front end of the critical inquiry as an orienting category for critical investigation of material. We will return to these matters after a brief rehearsal of Childs's life and career.

The Making of a Curious and Creative Scholar

Brevard Childs was born on September 2, 1923, in Columbia, South Carolina. The home Childs lived in for the first five years of his life was owned by his maternal grandfather, the president of a Columbia bank. Childs's

---

4. John Barton, *The Nature of Biblical Criticism* (Louisville: Westminster John Knox, 2007).

father, Richard, described the old man as "the last Confederate."[5] His Southern home had Methodist and Episcopalian roots. While in Columbia, the Childs family attended an Episcopal church. Though the majority of Childs's life took place in the Northeast, the gentle manner of a Southern aristocrat marked his professional manner and outlook. Childs was a generous and gracious man.

During the summer of 1929, the family moved to Flushing, New York, where Brevard's father took a position on Wall Street. The irony of the timing was not lost on Brevard, who said later, "Some timing," in reference to the stock market crash.[6] At first, the Childs family attended an Episcopal church in Flushing, but it was too "high church" for their taste. Upon hearing that a Southerner pastored the Presbyterian church, the family joined and became Presbyterian "by accident."[7] After graduating from high school in 1941, he attended Queens College in Flushing for a little over a year before joining the Army during World War II. Childs enlisted in October 1942 and spent a little over two years on the European front of the war. Surrounded by craps tables and gambling on the RMS *Queen Mary*, Childs taught himself Greek on the way to war.[8] This dogged determination is indicative of the endurance and energy that marked Childs's professional life.

After the war, Childs earned his undergraduate degree from the University of Michigan in 1947. In the same year, he entered graduate theological studies at Princeton Theological Seminary in Princeton, New Jersey. During his time there, Childs studied under such notables as Bruce Metzger and Otto Piper. According to Roy Harrisville and Walter Sundberg, Childs recognized in retrospect that "only a few, largely negative influences" can be traced to his time at Princeton Seminary.[9] Upon completion of his Bachelor of Divinity (1950), he pursued doctoral studies at the University of Basel, Switzerland. Though the University of Basel was best known for its theologian Karl Barth, Childs went to Basel for different reasons. He went to study Old Testament.[10]

---

5. Cited in Roy A. Harrisville and Walter Sundberg, *The Bible in Modern Culture: Baruch Spinoza to Brevard Childs* (Grand Rapids: Eerdmans, 2002), 309.

6. Ibid.

7. Ibid.

8. Daniel R. Driver, *Brevard Childs, Biblical Theologian: For the Church's One Bible* (Forschungen zum Alten Testament. 2. Reihe; Tübingen: Mohr Siebeck, 2010), 12–13.

9. Harrisville and Sundberg, *The Bible in Modern Culture*, 310.

10. Driver, *Brevard Childs, Biblical Theologian*, 13.

Old Testament scholarship at the universities in Switzerland and Germany was flourishing during this period. Childs initially studied under Walther Eichrodt, who is best known for his two-volume *Theology of the Old Testament*. During Childs's tenure at Basel, he took a year's study at Heidelberg, focusing on ancient Near Eastern studies. There Childs sat under Gerhard von Rad, but focused his attention on the nuts and bolts of Old Testament studies. Childs commented later in his preface to *Biblical Theology of the Old and New Testaments*, "It now seems ironical to recall that I spent more time in Heidelberg learning Arabic than listening to von Rad and [Günther] Bornkamm."[11]

Childs had the misfortune of being caught in the fray of a disagreement between two professors, Eichrodt and Walter Baumgartner. Childs submitted his thesis titled *Myth as a Theological Problem in the Old Testament* during a transition of power in the Old Testament department (1953); Baumgartner was replacing Eichrodt as senior Old Testament scholar. As is often the case on theology faculties, Eichrodt and Baumgartner had strongly different views about the methodology Childs deployed in his dissertation. Even though the faculty had formally accepted Childs's dissertation, Baumgartner refused to accept it in its current state and required substantial revisions.[12]

This was a devastating blow, as anyone who has given a doctoral defense knows. When Karl Barth heard about the fiasco, he called Childs into his office and gave him a set of inscribed books as an expression of condolence. Childs had to return to Basel to make the corrections to the thesis. As a concession to Childs, they allowed him to write the revision in English. It appeared in 1955 under the title *A Study of Myth in Genesis 1–11*. The material was revised a third time, appearing in 1960 in published form as *Myth and Reality in the Old Testament*.[13] In the preface to this work, Childs thanks both Eichrodt and Baumgartner for their help and influence

---

11. Brevard S. Childs, *Biblical Theology of the Old and New Testaments: Theological Reflection on the Christian Bible* (Minneapolis: Fortress, 1992), xv.

12. Daniel Driver's work on Brevard Childs (*Brevard Childs, Biblical Theologian*, 40–41) helpfully clarifies the details and chronology of this period in Childs's life. Driver procured a letter from Brevard Childs's mother to her daughter in which she provided details of these difficult days in Childs's life. From this letter, it seems Childs took the news in stride, while his mother said of the circumstances, "It just makes me sick." Driver also corrects some of the minor errors in detail found in Gerald Sheppard's account of Childs during this period. The journalistic side of Driver's work on Childs is a great aid to those wishing to know his intellectual history.

13. Brevard S. Childs, *Myth and Reality in the Old Testament* (Studies in Biblical Theology 27; London: SCM Press, 1960).

on the volume. In the preface to his *Exodus* commentary (1974), Childs says, "My academic interest in the book of Exodus goes back some twenty years ago to an unforgettable seminar on Moses which was conducted by Professor Walter Baumgartner of Basel in the summer semester of 1952."[14] If there was ill will toward Eichrodt (who according to Childs's mother shouldered more blame than Baumgartner) or Baumgartner, it was not in Childs's character to display it.

Childs consistently remembered his teachers and honored them in the prefaces of his many books. Though Eichrodt and Baumgartner were principal figures in his education at Basel, Childs mentions Gerhard von Rad, Walther Zimmerli, Oscar Cullmann, Günther Bornkamm, and others as well. His appreciation for these towering figures in his life did not dampen with the passing of years, even when he found it necessary to critique his teachers for the theological dead end of their methods. A telling commentary on Childs's self-understanding in relation to his teachers is found in the preface to his *Old Testament Theology in a Canonical Context*:

> I recall with gratitude the privilege of having heard lectures on Old Testament theology from my unforgettable teachers, W. Eichrodt, G. von Rad, and W. Zimmerli. In those places where I have been forced to register my disagreement, it is done in the spirit of honest theological inquiry which is a concern first learned from them. In the end, my sense of continuity with these great scholars of the church exceeds that of rupture.[15]

We will explore the significance of this statement when we turn specifically to the character of Childs's approach to Old Testament interpretation.

During his time at Basel, Childs met his wife, Ann, in Karl Barth's English-speaking seminar. This is an ironic providence in Childs's life because it should be remembered that Childs went to Basel to study Old Testament. Only later did Barth's influence on Childs become more apparent as he struggled to tear down the iron curtain separating biblical studies from Christian dogmatics. In a memorial colloquium held in 1969 at Yale Divinity School, Childs gave a humorous anecdote about attending Barth's lectures. Childs described a "biblical phalanx" that would sit together in

---

14. Brevard S. Childs, *The Book of Exodus: A Critical, Theological Commentary* (Old Testament Library; Philadelphia: Westminster, 1974), x.

15. Brevard S. Childs, *Old Testament Theology in a Canonical Context* (Philadelphia: Fortress, 1986), xiii.

the back of Barth's lectures, armed with Greek and Hebrew Bibles. When Childs was a student at Basel, the sentiment among the biblical studies students was that the only people who studied dogmatics were those who could not handle the Hebrew and the Greek.[16] Apparently, Barth was aware of this phalanx in the back and would occasionally look over at them, saying, "Not that I don't know all about J, E, D, and P," and then go on with his lectures as if he couldn't care less.[17]

Childs's first academic post in 1954 was at the Mission House Seminary in Wisconsin, a seminary no longer in existence. In 1958, he accepted a position at Yale Divinity School, where he taught until his retirement in 1999 as the Sterling Professor of Divinity. Childs was tireless in his studies and scholarly production. He produced a couple of smaller monographs on the front end of his career at Yale — *Memory and Tradition in Israel* and *Isaiah and the Assyrian Crisis*. In these works, Childs displays his ability to exegete the biblical text in the tradition-historical framework of his training received in Basel and Heidelberg.

In 1970, he wrote a landmark work titled *Biblical Theology in Crisis*. In this work, Childs gives an account of why the biblical theology movement of the 1950s and 1960s came undone in a rapid succession of events. James Barr's work *The Semantics of Biblical Language* revealed the faulty linguistic ground on which the movement rested. Langdon Gilkey's article "Cosmology, Ontology, and the Travail of Biblical Language" blew the whistle on the movement's equivocation regarding the reality of God's mighty acts in history. Pressures internal and external to the movement brought it to an end.[18]

Central to Childs's concern in *Biblical Theology in Crisis* is the overcoming of the strong dichotomy between biblical theology and Christian dogmatics. Childs registers strong resistance to identifying biblical theology as a descriptive task built on the back of the historical-critical project and theology as a prescriptive task that moves into territory less secure and more slippery than the assured results of objective exegesis.[19]

---

16. David L. Dickerman, ed., *Karl Barth and the Future of Theology: A Memorial Colloquium Held at Yale Divinity School, January 28, 1969* (New Haven, Conn.: Yale Divinity School Association, 1969), 30.

17. Ibid. For more on the relationship between Childs and Barth, see Driver, *Brevard Childs, Biblical Theologian*, chapter 3.

18. Brevard Childs, *Biblical Theology in Crisis* (Philadelphia: Westminster, 1970), 87.

19. This polarization of biblical theology and Christian dogmatics is demonstrated in Krister Stendahl's famous article on biblical theology in *The Interpreter's Dictionary of the Bible*, 1:418 – 32.

There is little hope of the biblical and theological disciplines interacting in a beneficial way unless biblical scholars are working constructively in theology, and conversely challenging the theologians to come to grips with the material described by the biblical disciplines. The proposal is not implying that the traditional division between biblical and dogmatic theology be abandoned, but rather suggesting that to have an area of overlap can aid in creating a genuine dialogue. It simply will not do to limit biblical theology to the descriptive task.[20]

In this book, the groundwork is laid for what would in time become the canonical approach.[21]

Childs was ever the learner. As a young professor at Yale Divinity School, he studied Akkadian under Albrecht Goetze. This is impressive, especially in light of the fact that Childs did no published work in comparative philology. Nevertheless, he studied Akkadian. He mentions in the preface to his *Biblical Theology of the Old and New Testaments* that he took the opportunity to study rabbinics for four semesters under Judah Goldin. Again, Childs was already a professor by this time. He then spent a year's sabbatical pursuing the same subject in Jerusalem. What Childs's continuing studies reveal was that his postgraduate work was in-service training, preparing him for a lifelong endeavor to learn and to learn thoroughly. Childs's intellectual curiosity would not allow him to remain on a straight and narrow disciplinary path dictated to him by the guild. Childs was creative and curious — a strong combination that led to groundbreaking work.

Childs remembered Barth's intimidating thoroughness in his research and writing. "Anyone who has ever studied under Karl Barth is left with the lasting sense of inadequacy just from remembering the standards of thoroughness which he required of his students."[22] A flip through the pages of Barth's *Church Dogmatics* illustrates the breadth and depth of Barth's engagement with the Christian tradition, biblical studies, and the history of ideas. Much like Barth, Childs was painstakingly thorough in his work, even when he recognized the difficulty of mastering the panoply of disciplines related to the one theological task.[23] As Childs described

---

20. Childs, *Biblical Theology in Crisis*, 93.

21. Childs (*Biblical Theology in Crisis*, 99 – 100) states, "Implied in the use of canon as a context for interpreting Scripture is a rejection of the method that would imprison the Bible within a context of the historical past."

22. Childs, *Biblical Theology of the Old and New Testaments*, xvi.

23. See Childs's preface to his *Exodus* commentary.

Barth's demanding thoroughness, Childs's students rehearse the same character trait in him. Christopher Seitz and Kathryn Greene-McCreight report the following:

> Alongside the drive for comprehension stood discipline and close attention to the constraints of scholarly publication. Who else would (or could) follow up a massive volume on biblical theology, in which matters seemingly so peripheral to the discipline of Old Testament studies were considered, such as ethics, preaching, and patristics, with the sort of technical writing typical of standard scholarly journals? And for those of us who were his doctoral students, who may have been privately dubious of or even openly antagonistic toward his challenges to the field, knew him to be the most formidable controller of those disciplines he was challenging. No one in the field would have entertained his more comprehensive proposals had they not been grounded in exegesis of the most careful, technical, and judicious sort and in the fullest possible conversation with historical-critical endeavor. And, to our horror, we knew that we were held to the same high standards that he held for himself.[24]

Childs was not content to remain in the academic ghetto of his own discipline. His scholarly work challenged assumed approaches to biblical studies as he crossed disciplinary boundaries for the sake of hearing the Christian Bible well.

Brevard Childs was a gracious and humble man. His critical knife cut sharp when engaging the work of others, but he never resorted to ad hominem attacks or a self-referential egocentricity about his own work. Childs rarely assigned his own published material in the courses he taught. It was not in his personal makeup to be self-referential in public or in private. Seitz and Greene-McCreight write, "Childs was immune to egocentric rigidity on the one hand and to the winds of changing doctrine on the other because of a character of humility grounded in the desire for, above all else in his life and work, obedience to God's Word."[25] Because of this devotion to obedience to Scripture, Childs's students saw the combustive

---

24. Christopher Seitz and Kathryn Greene-McCreight, eds., *Theological Exegesis: Essays in Honor of Brevard S. Childs* (Grand Rapids: Eerdmans, 1999), 4–5. In 2004, I met with Brevard Childs in his Cambridge, England, flat. I noticed a Berlitz guide to Italian on the table, and when I asked him about this, he said he was brushing up on his Italian for a trip he and Ann were taking. He was in his early eighties and still learning Italian.

25. Ibid., 5.

combination of prayer, preaching, and exegesis in the service of God's Word.[26] Childs passed away on June 23, 2007, after suffering from a fall.

The scope of Childs's work is impressive by anyone's standards — scholarly articles, commentaries, discipline-altering introductions to the Old and New Testament (though the latter volume had a stillbirth among New Testament scholars), a work on Old Testament theology, and a culminating biblical theology in 1992. Subsequent to this volume, Childs produced a commentary on Isaiah, a history of interpretation of Isaiah, and, frustrated with the way Pauline scholars had framed the issue, a work on the canonical shaping and significance of the Pauline corpus. Childs's indefatigable energy and broad scholarly interests call to mind the great scholars of the past who had complete control of their own discipline and could move seamlessly into others as well — figures such as W. M. L. de Wette and Julius Wellhausen. In contrast to these figures, however, Childs's work traversed the Testaments, dipped into Christian theology, and struggled with the history of interpretation because he believed the material form of Scripture and the role in the divine economy it demanded. Daniel Driver is right to describe Childs as a biblical theologian and leave this description loose enough to account for the multifaceted character of Childs's approach. Keeping in mind the aims and intentions of this volume, a full account of Childs's contribution as a biblical theologian will not be pursued.[27] Our attention will remain focused on his critical Old Testament work and the way the canonical approach situates itself both confessionally and critically.

The Canonical Approach:
Confessional and Critical

Childs resisted the term *canon criticism* as an apt description of his approach. On this account, canon criticism is relegated to a list of other criticisms (*Geschichten*), such as source, form, or redaction. Yet Childs did not understand the canonical approach as another option in the growing list of critical approaches. In an interview, Childs gives his reasons for preferring "canonical approach" over against "canon criticism":

---

26. Ibid.

27. For a full account of these matters see Christopher R. Seitz, *Word without End: The Old Testament as Abiding Theological Witness* (Grand Rapids: Eerdmans, 1998), chapter 9; Driver, *Brevard Childs, Biblical Theologian.*

I have always objected to the term "canon(ical) criticism" as a suitable description of my approach. I do not envision my approach as involving a new critical methodology analogous to literary, form, or redactional criticism. Rather, the crucial issue turns on one's initial evaluation of the nature of the biblical text being studied. By defining one's task as an understanding of the Bible as the sacred Scriptures of the church, one establishes from the outset the context and point-of-understanding of the reader within the received tradition of a community of faith and practice.[28]

Childs's canonical approach is not a detached investigation of critical issues in Old Testament studies or a mere historical description of Jewish and Christian understandings of canon. It is an approach whose warrant rests in a confessional understanding of the nature and role of the biblical material in the communities of faith that treasured and preserved them for future generations of believers.

At the same time, Childs's approach is located in modernity and would not be conceivable in the form in which he presents it without an appreciative, even if critical, nod in the direction of modern biblical criticism. Childs's approach is modern in much the same way that Barth is a theologian of modernity. The critical challenges of modernity are respected as a challenge and an opportunity.[29] For Childs, modernity's handling of the Bible and the methods spawned from it are both to be appreciated and brought under critical scrutiny. It is not an option to turn a blind eye from what has been discovered with these methods, despite the negligible sources of the discovery. Childs does not fall prey to the genetic fallacy; that is, something is inherently wrong because of its tainted beginnings or source. His approach is not a precritical or premodern repristination of methods located on the near side of modernity; Calvin and Luther come back to life.[30] Rather, Childs is located on the far side of the

---

28. "An Interview with Brevard S. Childs (1923–2007)," www.philosophy-religion.org/Bible/Childs-Interview.Htm; see also Childs, *Introduction to the Old Testament as Scripture*, 82–83.

29. Bruce McCormack gave a collection of his published essays on Barth the title *Orthodox and Modern*.

30. Though Childs's appreciation for premodern interpreters should not be attenuated. As early as 1970, Childs stated, "When our seminary-trained pastors find Augustine incomprehensible, Luther verbose, and Calvin dull, then obviously the problem lies with the reader and his theological education and not with the old masters" (*Biblical Theology in Crisis*, 147). See also his work on the history of interpretation of Isaiah (*The Struggle to Understand Isaiah as Christian Scripture* [Grand Rapids: Eerdmans, 2004]).

historical-critical project. He takes some cues while resisting others when negotiating its conclusions and claims.

It is important to recognize that Childs is willing to grant much to the historical-critical project and the "depth dimension" it has discovered in the biblical texts — depth dimension refers to the complex literary layers present in the final form of biblical books; these layers of tradition are deciphered by the critical tools given by source, form, and tradition criticism in particular. As noted in the biographical section of this chapter, Childs understood his approach to Old Testament criticism and theology more in continuity with his teachers Gerhard von Rad and Walther Zimmerli than discontinuous with them. Childs assumes the biblical books of the Old Testament are the products of a very long and complex compositional history:

> The final canonical literature reflects a long history of development in which the received tradition was selected, transmitted, and shaped by hundreds of decisions. This process of construing its religious tradition involved a continual critical evaluation of historical options which were available to Israel and a transformation of its received tradition toward certain theological goals. That the final form of the biblical text has preserved much from the earlier stages of Israel's theological reflection is fully evident.[31]

Both form criticism's move to locate literary genres and traditions in a preliterary social-religious context and tradition criticism's focus on the ongoing reception and transmission of these traditions in the literary deposits of Israel's religious life provide Childs the critical tools necessary to recognize a "depth dimension" in the final form of biblical books. This is often an unsung note in rehearsing Childs's canonical approach. It is important to understand the high regard Childs had for these critical discoveries.

At the same time, Childs registered a strong complaint about the use of these critical tools when they shift attention away to the text's preliterary stages or historical reconstruction. Childs is appreciative of the advances of tradition criticism. Nevertheless, he warns about three deleterious tendencies of tradition criticism. First, the level of confidence and interpretive necessity attached to the discovery of the depth dimension (a text's

---

31. Childs, *Old Testament Theology in a Canonical Context*, 11.

diachronic history) is overshot. Childs writes, "The various elements have been so fused as to resist easy diachronic reconstructions which fracture the witness as a whole."[32] Recognition of a complex tradition-historical process leading to the text's final form and confidence in reconstructing this history are two different matters for Childs. Again, Childs clarifies, "By assuming the normative status of the final form of the text, the canonical approach evokes the strongest opposition from the side of traditio-historical criticism *for which the heart of the exegetical task is the recovery of the depth dimension*" (emphasis mine).[33]

Second, Childs denies the coequal status given to the identified levels of tradition and the text's final form:

> The controversy with traditio-historical critics is not over the theological significance of a depth dimension of the tradition. Rather, the issue turns on whether or not features within the tradition which have subordinated, modified, or placed in the distant background of the text can be interpreted apart from the role assigned to them in the final form when attempting to write a theology of the Old Testament.[34]

We will return to this matter, but it is worth stating here that the final form of the biblical books leaves an important and necessary interpretive imprint on the material that is lost when the text is fragmented and read against its own grain.

Third, Childs is dubious about approaches to the biblical material that do not allow canon to play a constitutive role in our understanding and use of the critical issues in Old Testament interpretation. In short, Childs is critically appreciative of critical approaches to Old Testament interpretation, while in the final analysis he finds critical approaches anemic when attending to the theological character of the Old Testament as Scripture.

As a side note, it is worth mentioning that Childs's project is also modern because it resists reader-response theories that locate meaning in the self-discovery of the community as the text itself is swallowed by the community's interest (even though Childs has much to say about the important role the community of faith plays as tradents of the material, i.e., those responsible for preserving and passing on the oral tradition). Childs still holds on to a notion of intentionality, though intentionality is not located

---

32. Ibid.
33. Childs, *Introduction to the Old Testament as Scripture*, 75.
34. Childs, *Old Testament Theology in a Canonical Context*, 11.

in isolating the various components of composite texts and deciphering the original situation out of which those texts arose, as in Hermann Gunkel. For Childs, intentionality is located in the canonical shaping of the material — a shaping that includes the final form of the book and the arrangement of the material. Thus, the depth dimension may shed light on the final form of the material, but Childs does not allow the identified depth dimension (which is always proximate, never final, and often speculative) to be the goal for deciphering intentionality. In this sense, intentionality has a broader scope of reference that takes into account the way the book in its final form associates with itself (e.g., there is no Deutero-Isaiah in Isaiah) and with other books in the canonical corpus (e.g., Exodus 34 and the final shaping of the Book of the Twelve). Childs's project is a modern one and cannot be conceived of outside the parameters established by modernity's handling of the Bible (source criticism, form criticism, tradition criticism, redaction criticism). At the same time, Childs's canonical approach seeks to avoid the hubris, naturalism, and scientific optimism that have plagued the discipline. It is almost enough to remind the reader of the title of Child's groundbreaking work — *Introduction to the Old Testament as Scripture.*

Two terms continue to surface in our overview of Childs's canonical approach. The first is *canon.* And the second is *final form.* For the sake of providing some handles on this approach, I will take a closer look at these two terms and how they function in this approach.

Canon in Childs's Framework

The theological notion of canon plays a material role in Childs's interpretive schema. In fact, the general acceptance or rejection of the canonical approach trades on how one understands and defines the term. For Childs, the appeal to canon cannot be limited to an external decision made by the synagogue or church in which the scope of the canon is defined and closed. On this account, canon becomes a formal quality of the Old Testament and is reduced to an understanding of canon as list. The synagogue or the church determines which books are in the list of authoritative writings, and thus the canon becomes "closed" after this decision is made. Because this decision regarding the scope of the canon is external to the material itself, it exerts no pressure when interpreting the Old Testament documents in their various historical contexts and compositional history.

Childs's friend A. C. Sundberg wrote an informed and influential study on the Old Testament in the early church and suggested a conceptual distinction between canon — implying a closed collection — and Scripture — a body of authoritative writings.[35] Childs found this distinction too crystalline because it did not take into account the embedded canon consciousness present in the formation of the biblical literature itself; it was not simply a tack-on at the end. He makes this statement:

> In my judgment, to conceive of canon mainly as a dogmatic decision regarding the scope of the literature is to overestimate one feature within the process which is, by no means, constitutive of canon. Moreover, the sharp distinction obscures some of the most important features in the development of canon by limiting the term only to the final stages of a long and complex process which had already started in the preexilic period.[36]

The distinction between Scripture and canon, for Childs, obscures important forces at work in the period of writing and shaping the biblical literature.

The interaction between the growing corpus of authoritative literature and the community that valued it is "essential to understanding the growth of canon," according to Childs.[37] The individuals and community involved in the writing, shaping, and transmission of the biblical documents recognized their inspired and authoritative status. This canonical recognition, or canon consciousness as Childs calls it, exerted a pressure on the writing and formation of the literature itself. For example, one sees a canon consciousness present in Isaiah 8:16 and 31:8, where the prophet calls for his message to be recorded for the sake of a future generation. Similarly, in the New Testament, we hear the apostle Paul refer to the Old Testament as having been written "to teach us" (Romans 15:3). Embedded in the Scriptures' own self-referencing is a consciousness of its canonical role as an intended Word for future generations of the faithful.

The formation of the Old Testament material, therefore, into a canonical norm was not a late extrinsic matter only — Childs prefers the term *canonization* to refer to the final fixing of the scope of Scripture — but was

---

35. A. C. Sundberg, *The Old Testament of the Early Church* (Cambridge: Cambridge Univ. Press, 1964).

36. Brevard S. Childs, "The Exegetical Significance of Canon for the Study of the Old Testament," in *Congress Volume: Göttingen 1977*, ed. J. A. Emerton, et al. (Supplements to Vetus Testamentum 29; Leiden: Brill, 1978), 67.

37. Ibid.

an intrinsic matter at play in the actual compositional history of the biblical books and component parts of the Old Testament witness (Law, Prophets, and Writings). Childs recognizes other aspects at work in the history of the Hebrew literature, e.g., literary patterns, social situations, scribal techniques, and so forth. Still, the recognition of the sacred and authoritative nature of the Old Testament documents was integral not only to their later reception but also their literary and compositional history.

Accordingly, Childs defines canon as follows: "That historical process within ancient Israel — particularly in the postexilic period — which entailed a collecting, selecting, and ordering of texts to serve a normative function as Sacred Scripture within the continuing religious continuity."[38] It is noteworthy that Childs appeals to "history" here. In other words, the canonical approach is concerned about the historical character of the biblical literature as well. But Childs's appeal to history is canonically conceived, as it takes into account the "collecting, selecting, and ordering of texts" into a final literary form and canonical shape. Childs warns, "Nevertheless, it is a basic misunderstanding of the canonical approach to describe it as a non-historical reading of the Bible. Nothing could be further from the truth! Rather, the issue at stake is the nature of the Bible's historicality and the search for a historical approach that is commensurate with it."[39] The canonical approach does appeal to a kind of history that coalesces with a sacred understanding of the literature's nature. The appeal to history, however, is not limited to the genetic history of the biblical books alone: e.g., original author and original audience historically or redactionally reconstructed. Childs was less than hopeful about the confidence attached to deciphering the diachronic history of biblical books.

Childs follows his definition of canon with this clarifying explanation:

> In the transmission process, traditions which once arose in a particular milieu and were addressed to various historical situations were shaped in such a way as to serve as a normative expression of God's will to later generations of Israel who had not shared in those original historical events.[40]

Embedded in Childs's understanding of canon and the pressure it exerted on the development of the biblical material is a commitment to the

---

38. Ibid.
39. Childs, *Introduction to the Old Testament as Scripture*, 71.
40. Childs, "Exegetical Significance of Canon," 67.

enduring witness of the Old Testament as a divine word that goes beyond the historical situation out of which the material arose. This is a crux in the canonical approach. To illustrate from hermeneutics, the distinction between meaning (what a text said in its original historical context as discovered by rigorous historical and grammatical investigation) and significance (the way this text is received as an authoritative word beyond its historical genesis) does not work. In fact, the canonical process itself exhibits the falseness of this distinction: "Let this be written for a future generation" (Psalm 102:18). When biblical books are arranged and shaped into the form in which Israel and the church have received them, they are loosed from their historical moorings so as to function as an ongoing vehicle for divine communication. This point is further elaborated in the second of our two handles on the canonical approach, namely, Childs's privileging of the final form.

The Final Form of the Text

Childs privileges the final form and canonical shaping of the Old Testament documents for historical and theological reasons, both of which flow from the particular relationship of the community of faith with the canonical documents. The historical reason Childs insists on privileging the final form relates to the historical encounter between Israel and God that is reflected in the biblical text. God revealed himself to Israel in various ways (Hebrews 1:1) in real time and space. For Childs, "Canon serves to describe this peculiar relationship and to define the scope of this history by establishing a beginning and an end to the process."[41] These encounters between Israel and God witnessed to in the biblical text reflect a special and unique quality of Israel's history. The reception of these accounts into the biblical canon requires this history to become a normative witness for future generations. Childs provides the following rationale for why the final form of the biblical documents is privileged over against the reconstruction of the layers of tradition leading up to the final form: "The significance of the final form of the biblical text is that it alone bears witness to the full history of revelation."[42] The final form of the biblical documents reflects the maturity, perspective, and scope of many generations of devotional and critical interaction with God's historical encounters with Israel.

---

41. Childs, *Introduction to the Old Testament as Scripture*, 75.
42. Ibid., 75–76.

In this sense, the final form functions as an authoritative commentary on the full scope of Israel's encounter with God. Childs clarifies, "It is only the final form of the biblical text in which the normative history has reached an end that the full effect of this revelatory history can be perceived."[43]

Furthermore for Childs, "Canon implies that the witness to Israel's experience with God lies not in the process, which has usually been lost or purposely blurred, but is testified to in the effect on the biblical text itself."[44] This is a crucial turn of phrase in the canonical approach. Two things are worth observing here. First, the biblical text itself is recognized as the location of God's self-revealing. This does not in any way attenuate the real time and space encounters God had with his people in history. But "history per se is not a medium of revelation which is commensurate with canon."[45] The biblical texts themselves provide a normative perspective and understanding of the historical events. Thus, the biblical texts are the locus of revelation and not the events in and of themselves apart from God's revealed wisdom regarding their significance. It is a wrong turn, according to Childs, to seek a historical reconstruction behind the text itself precisely because such an effort runs roughshod over the privileged and revealed canonical take on these events.

Second, the final form of the biblical documents leaves a hermeneutical imprint on the material that renders an authoritative judgment regarding the text's prehistory. Childs's approach is the complete opposite of Julius Wellhausen's "the half is more than the whole." For Childs, the whole, or final canonical shape, is more than the sum of its parts — J, E, D, and P's independent literary sources now singing solos next to each other. Rather, "the full, combined text has rendered a judgment on the shape of the tradition which continues to exert its authority on the community of faith."[46] Though the prehistory of the Pentateuch may allow for a more precise hearing of the Pentateuch, the final form of the Pentateuch fashions this prehistory into a unified whole (however frustrating that whole may be) that now creates its own harmonious voice — a different matter than hearing four solos.

---

43. Ibid., 76.

44. Childs, "Exegetical Significance of Canon," 69.

45. Childs, *Introduction to the Old Testament as Scripture*, 76. In the conclusion I will briefly refer to Karl Barth's claim that "revelation is not a predicate of history, but history is a predicate of revelation." Childs's comments here relate to Barth's concern.

46. Ibid.

Herein lies Childs's theological commitment to the texts themselves as God's means of continued self-revelation. For example, the unified five books of the Pentateuch are sacred Scripture for Jews and Christians in this particular form and not in a refracted analysis of the prehistory leading up to this form. To take another well-known critical matter, Isaiah's complex compositional history (a complex history Childs affirms) is not what is presented in the final canonical shape and form of Isaiah as a sixty-six-chapter whole. To read Isaiah as something other than a literary unity is to not read the canonical Isaiah Jews and Christians have received as sacred Scripture. Though there may have been a historical "Deutero-Isaiah," the final form of Isaiah's prophetic voice has rendered a historical identification of this figure impossible.

Childs states this conclusion:

> Again, to take canon seriously is also to take seriously the critical function which it exercises in respect to earlier stages of the literature's formation. A critical judgment is evidenced in the way in which these earlier stages are handled. At times the original material is passed on unchanged; at other times the tradents have selected, rearranged, or expanded the received tradition. The role of canon is to bring to bear a critical theological judgment on the process which is exercised in fixing a final shape to the literature.[47]

The commitment to canon and final form is both historical and theological. In the final analysis, however, the theological commitment shapes Childs's understanding of the historical as well. Childs willingly recognizes the historical and social forces at work in the production of the biblical documents. But his understanding of canon does not flow from the bottom up.[48] Rather, the historical forces at work in the production of the biblical material are understood through the theological prism of revelation and providence. These two theological loci govern the whole approach. Without them the project would collapse.

Let me briefly illustrate Childs's canonical approach by drawing attention to his appreciative critique of Walther Zimmerli's critical reading of Ezekiel. Zimmerli's work on Ezekiel yielded two macro-exegetical results.

---

47. Childs, "Exegetical Significance of Canon," 69.

48. James A. Sanders's understanding of canon follows this path. See his *Torah and Canon*, 2nd ed. (Eugene, Ore.: Cascade, 2005) and *Canon and Community: A Guide to Canonical Criticism* (Eugene, Ore.: Wipf & Stock, 2000).

First, he demonstrates the special features of Ezekiel's prophetic speech by a masterly use of form and traditio-critical methods. Ezekiel's prophetic words are shown to be dependent on ancient Hebrew traditions and located in a social-legal situation that closely parallels the Holiness Code of Leviticus (chs. 17 – 26). Second, Zimmerli focuses on the "afterlife" (*Nachinterpretation*) of the prophetic speeches in an effort to demonstrate how the book's various levels of growth resulted in the final form. An original Ezekiel kernel (*Grundtext*) was accepted and expanded by a post-exilic school.[49] Childs believes Zimmerli's work represents a real advance in addressing the critical problems of the book. Here the appreciative note is rung. Zimmerli's form and traditio-critical analysis has yielded important results for our understanding of Ezekiel's compositional history.

Where Childs demurs, however, is the direction Zimmerli moves once this critical history has been identified:

> Nevertheless, in my judgment, there are some inadequacies in Zimmerli's commentary. Above all, I do not think that he has correctly assessed the canonical shape of the book, but has rested his interpretation on a critically reconstructed precanonical form of the book. In this regard he has retained too close a continuity with the assumptions of the historical critical methodology.[50]

Zimmerli's critical handling of Ezekiel is right in the recognition of a lengthy canonical process leading to the text's final form. He is wrong, though, in focusing his efforts on establishing the precanonical stage in an effort at isolating the original oracles (*Grundtext*) on which the "afterlife" of the text is based. What, in effect, happens on this account is that all the canonical material not identified as original oracles becomes commentary on the real text of Ezekiel, the text Zimmerli has critically reconstructed.

The problems on this account are threefold. First, Zimmerli's approach downplays the continuity between the original oracles and their afterlife. The original prophetic word is played over against the continued life of this prophetic word beyond the historical prophet per se in this particular and extended moment in Israel's history before God. Second, Zimmerli attenuates the significant role the final canonical shape plays in ordering the material in a single theological voice all related to Ezekiel's prophetic

---

49. Childs, *Introduction to the Old Testament as Scripture*, 359 – 60.
50. Ibid., 360.

word. Third, Zimmerli assumes the governing norm of historical-critical interpretation, namely, that the historical reconstruction of the text is necessary in aiding and illuminating interpretation. To fragment the book according to its traditio-historical reconstruction is to lose the canonical force of the book as a literary whole in its final form. Again, one observes with Childs his appreciation of Zimmerli's critical achievements, while at the same time calling into question the fundamental assumptions of the method's operating goals.

Conclusion

The paradigm shift of Childs's approach brought with it multiple criticisms from various quadrants of biblical and theological studies. Paul Noble suggests Childs's approach needs a firmer commitment to the doctrine of inspiration and a historical outlook that asks, "What really happened?" James Barr, Childs's long-standing critic, continuously declared his belief that Childs did not know his own mind, confusing both himself and his readers.[51] Others, such as John Barton, sought to dampen Childs's voice by associating him with literary approaches now deemed deficient. Mark Brett worries that Childs's approach cannot avoid the charge of fideism, nor can it give an account of the canonical editors' motives, which are necessary to understand the canonical final form (according to Brett, not Childs).[52]

Evangelical voices (John Piper, Carl F. H. Henry, Ian Provan) reacted in a critically appreciative way, worrying whether or not Childs attenuates the historical referentiality of the Bible or whether he sold the farm in his own appreciation of the achievement of historical criticism.[53] And from the theological side, R. R. Reno questions whether or not Childs's particular hermeneutical approach falls prey to overplaying the distinction between

---

51. James Barr, *The Concept of Biblical Theology: An Old Testament Perspective* (Minneapolis: Fortress, 1999), 378–438.

52. Mark G. Brett, *Biblical Criticism in Crisis? The Impact of the Canonical Approach on Old Testament Studies* (Cambridge: Cambridge Univ. Press, 1991). See Childs's comments on the difference between the concerns of redaction criticism and the canonical approach ("Exegetical Significance of Canon," 68–69).

53. John Piper, "Authority and Meaning in the Christian Canon: A Response to Gerald Sheppard on Canon Criticism," *Journal of the Evangelical Theological Society* 19 (1976): 87–96; Carl F. H. Henry, "Canonical Theology: An Evangelical Appraisal," *Scottish Bulletin of Theology* 8 (1990): 76–108; Ian Provan, "Canons to the Left of Him: Brevard Childs, His Critics, and the Future of Old Testament Theology," *Scottish Journal of Theology* 50 (1997): 1–38.

sign and reality.[54] It is beyond the scope of this chapter to engage all of the criticisms here, and there are more than these briefly mentioned.[55] Needless to say, Childs has been warmly received by some, hostilely rejected by others, and cautiously appreciated by many.

It is probably fair to observe that Childs was clear in his own mind about interpretive boundaries and when they were crossed in the hermeneutical process. He could be a rigorous critic of those who were, at the end of the day, in his camp (if such battle imagery is helpful). For example, he chides Walter Moberly for confusing midrashic with allegorical or figural intertextual readings in the Christian canon.[56] Hugh Williamson relies too much on the speculative side of redaction criticism in his work on Isaiah, though Childs himself makes much use of redaction-critical analysis in his Isaiah commentary.[57] Nicholas Wolterstorff leans on an alien philosophical category (speech-act theory) to rescue a doctrine of inspiration not really in need of this kind of rescuing.[58] All to say, Childs saw the biblical theological field clearly and could be a thorough critic when he thought biblical scholars or theologians were inching toward or heading down a wrong path. What might be too much spice for one may be just right for another. And Childs was gracious enough but happy to send the plate back to the kitchen.

These kinds of debates are the natural outcome of an approach that really is an approach and not a "method" per se. In fact, the canonical process has built within it a "dimension of flexibility which encourages constantly fresh ways of actualizing the material."[59] Theological parameters are set, yet the borderland may be fuzzy in the actual exegetical and theological task. Christopher Seitz accurately assesses, "Canonical reading is therefore not an exact science, but a theological decision about what the proper parameters for interpretation are: the final-form presentation and

---

54. R. R Reno, "Biblical Theology and Theological Exegesis," in *Out of Egypt: Biblical Theology and Biblical Interpretation*, ed. C. Bartholomew, et al. (Scripture and Hermeneutics 5; Grand Rapids: Zondervan, 2004), 385–408.

55. Daniel Driver's work on Childs (*Brevard Childs, Biblical Theologian*) addresses the major detractors to Childs's approach.

56. Brevard S. Childs, "Critique of Recent Intertextual Canonical Interpretation," *Zeitschrift für die Alttestamentliche Wissenschaft* 115 (2003): 173–84.

57. See Childs's comments on Isaiah 12 in his commentary on *Isaiah* (Old Testament Library; Louisville: Westminster John Knox, 2001).

58. Brevard S. Childs, "Speech-Act Theory and Biblical Interpretation," *Scottish Journal of Theology* 58 (2005): 375–92.

59. Childs, *Old Testament Theology in a Canonical Context*, 13.

the arrangement and sequencing that it exhibits, over against the simple history of the text's development as this is critically reconstructed."[60] Because it is not an exact science, debates will continue as the approach is deployed in the critical reading of Scripture. Yet the exegetical possibilities are numerous for those who confess the sacred character of the Old Testament, the priority of the final form, and the importance of reading biblical books/texts in canonical association with other biblical books/texts. All of these exegetical labors strive toward one end, namely, to hear the word of the Lord.

FOR FURTHER READING

Childs, Brevard S. *Biblical Theology of the Old and New Testaments: Theological Reflection on the Christian Bible*. Minneapolis: Fortress, 1992.

———. "Critique of Recent Intertextual Canonical Interpretation." *Zeitschrift für die Alttestamentliche Wissenschaft* 115 (2003): 173–84.

———. "The Exegetical Significance of Canon for the Study of the Old Testament." Pages 68–80 in *Congress Volume: Göttingen 1977*. Supplements to Vetus Testamentum 29. Edited J. A. Emerton, W. L. Holladay, A. Lemaire, R. E. Murphy, E. Nielsen, R. Smend, and J.A. Soggin. Leiden: Brill, 1978.

———. *Introduction to the Old Testament as Scripture*. Philadelphia: Fortress, 1979.

———. *Old Testament Theology in a Canonical Context*. Philadelphia: Fortress, 1985.

Driver, Daniel R. *Brevard Childs, Biblical Theologian: For the Church's One Bible*. Forschungen zum Alten Testament. 2. Reihe. Tübingen: Mohr Siebeck, 2010.

Provan, Ian. "Canons to the Left of Him: Brevard Childs, His Critics, and the Future of Old Testament Theology." *Scottish Journal of Theology* 50 (1997): 1–38.

continued on next page

---

60. Christopher Seitz, "Canonical Approach," in *Dictionary for Theological Interpretation of the Bible*, ed. Kevin J. Vanhoozer (Grand Rapids: Baker, 2005), 100–101.

Reno, R. R. "Biblical Theology and Theological Exegesis." Pages 385 – 408 in *Out of Egypt: Biblical Theology and Biblical Interpretation.* Scripture and Hermeneutics Series 5. Edited by C. Bartholomew, M. Healy, K. Möller, and R. Parry. Grand Rapids: Zondervan, 2004.

Seitz, Christopher R. *Word without End: The Old Testament as Abiding Theological Witness.* Grand Rapids: Eerdmans, 1998.

——. "Canonical Approach." Pages 100 – 102 in *Dictionary for Theological Interpretation of the Bible.* Edited by Kevin J. Vanhoozer. Grand Rapids: Baker, 2005.

——. "The Canonical Approach and Theological Interpretation." Pages 58 – 110 in *Canon and Biblical Interpretation.* Scripture and Hermeneutics Series 7. Edited by C. Bartholomew, S. Hahn, R. Parry, C. Seitz, and A. Wolters. Grand Rapids: Zondervan, 2006.

Seitz, Christopher, and Kathryn Greene-McCreight, eds. *Theological Exegesis: Essays in Honor of Brevard S. Childs.* Grand Rapids: Eerdmans, 1999.

Sheppard, Gerald T. "Childs, Brevard." Pages 301 – 10 in *Dictionary of Major Biblical Interpreters.* Edited by Donald K. McKim. Downers Grove, Ill.: InterVarsity, 2007.

MORE A POSTSCRIPT
THAN CONCLUSION

A BIRD'S-EYE VIEW OF THE HISTORY OF OLD TESTAMENT CRITICISM inevitably leaves gaps. As mentioned in the introduction, other figures could have been chosen to illustrate trends in the field. Brevard Childs came last in our picture gallery tour. Admittedly, this is shortsighted as well and does not take into account developments in postmodern approaches to biblical studies, feminist studies, postcolonial approaches, and a host of differing options arriving on the hermeneutical stage at a dizzying pace. As the reader can tell, I have high regard for the canonical approach and Brevard Childs. But hope is to be found in other quadrants of the scholarly and ecclesial world of Old Testament interpretation.

All the figures in this book are modern in the sense of their location in the history of ideas. Even Childs's project, which resists modern historicist tendencies, takes many of its cues and points of departure from the achievements of modern critical study of the Old Testament. In an effort at producing something accessible and manageable (to the reader and me!), I have kept to this particular stream of Old Testament criticism. All to say, this volume is meant to be a brief introduction to orient students and interested readers to the field while pointing them on to further study and inquiry. I hope this book will serve as this kind of catalyst.

There is one particular stream missing from this narrative that deserves to be mentioned in brief. Alongside the swelling tide of modern biblical criticism was a countervailing conservative voice and reaction. In some sense, William Foxwell Albright fits into this camp, and in another sense he does not. These conservative voices denied the naturalistic outlook often attached to modern biblical criticism and sought to defeat it by their own methods and stringent analysis of the biblical material. In the nineteenth century, Ernst Wilhelm Hengstenberg, who took the Old Testament chair vacated by W. M. L. de Wette at the University of Berlin, was a strong conservative voice arguing along exegetical and theological grounds for a Christian reading of the Old Testament. Hengstenberg's approach was apologetic in outlook and was not as neutral and self-evident as he may have thought. Still, Hengstenberg was a vociferous, learned, and politically shrewd figure who sought to quell the rise of biblical criticism in German university life. His efforts did not succeed. Similarly, Franz Delitzsch was a learned opponent of modern biblical criticism. In time, Delitzsch softened on some critical issues, such as the single authorship of Isaiah, but his outlook remained opposed to the naturalistic instincts often attached to modern criticism. Hengstenberg and Delitzsch differed in their level of openness to the spirit of the day. At the same time, both are representative of a confessional reaction against biblical methods beholden to deism, naturalism, and rationalism.

The old Princeton Seminary of the late nineteenth and early twentieth centuries housed several gifted and able critics of modern criticism. Joseph Alexander wrote a learned commentary on Isaiah arguing against an understanding of multiple authorship. This commentary reveals Alexander's impressive abilities in Semitics and Old Testament exegesis. William Henry Green was a fair and able opponent of Julius Wellhausen's reconstruction of Israel's religious history, even if his arguments against Wellhausen did not persuade the academy. This tradition continued with scholar-theologians such as Geerhardus Vos, O. T. Allis, and many other more recent figures who identify with J. Gresham Machen's original efforts at denominational and seminary reform. The role of Old Testament criticism in theological education and the church created great amounts of relational and ecclesial friction during the turn of the nineteenth century. This friction is illustrated in the lives of William Robertson Smith and the Free Church of Scotland, Charles Briggs and the Presbyterian Church, and Crawford Toy with the Southern Baptists.

The narrative of evangelical responses to modern biblical criticism is a long and complex story betraying simple outlines and codification. One would have to examine figures such as Gleason Archer and R. K. Harrison, both of whom were venerable and learned opponents of the assumptions and conclusions of modern biblical criticism. Following this narrative would demand another volume and take us down roads of theological and denominational controversies that are felt to this day.[1] But one unavoidable conclusion that does arise in this narrative is that biblical scholars of the confessional kind always walk a tightrope between their theological commitments and the results of modern biblical criticism.[2] When the scholar actually topples off the tightrope in a "liberal" or "conservative" direction is not as clearly defined as we may wish.

There are self-identified evangelical voices today calling for wholesale adoption of the assured results of modern biblical criticism on the basis of a theory of accommodation received from John Calvin himself.[3] More modest evangelical appropriations of critical conclusions can be found in Bruce Waltke's understanding of the compositional history of the Pentateuch extending into the exilic period.[4] John Sailhamer's recently expressed understanding of a Pentateuch-A (early form of the book) and Pentateuch-B (later exilic redaction) is an approach that affirms both Mosaic authorship and a complex compositional/redactional history at the same time.[5] The list of conservative voices wrestling with the material form of the Old Testament in light of their confession of faith and the difficult dialectic this creates could extend for some pages. All of this to say that if the conversation is to move forward, Christian virtue, good arguments, and theological instincts are all needed in spades. I will avoid analysis of these trends here and will simply state that the difficult relationship between confessional identity and modern biblical criticism is an issue that is alive and well.

It is worth reflecting a bit more on the necessary role one's Christian confession regarding the nature and role of Scripture plays in shaping our approach to reading and understanding it. In a trenchant analysis of Hans Frei's *The Eclipse of Biblical Narrative* — a watershed volume — Neil MacDonald expresses his reservation about Frei's use of "critical" and "precritical" as apt descriptors of the shift taking place with modern study of the

---

1. See the moving account of Fuller Seminary's history in George M. Marsden, *Reforming Fundamentalism: Fuller Seminary and the New Evangelicalism* (Grand Rapids: Eerdmans, 1987).

2. Mark A. Noll, *Between Faith and Criticism: Evangelicals, Scholarship, and the Bible in America* (Vancouver, B.C.: Regent College Publishing, 1991).

3. Noteworthy is Kenton L. Sparks, *God's Word in Human Words: An Evangelical Appropriation of Critical Biblical Scholarship* (Grand Rapids: Baker, 2008).

4. Bruce K. Waltke, *An Old Testament Theology: An Exegetical, Canonical, and Thematic Approach* (Grand Rapids: Zondervan, 2007), 56 – 58.

5. John H. Sailhamer, *The Meaning of the Pentateuch: Revelation, Composition and Interpretation* (Downers Grove, Ill.: InterVarsity, 2009).

Bible (seventeenth century onward).[6] He prefers "modern" and "premodern" because the other terms suggest a lack of critical inquiry into the Scriptures with premodern figures such as Augustine, Aquinas, Luther, or Calvin; this is simply not the case.

For MacDonald, what marks the shift between modern and premodern readers of Scripture is the placement of belief in their epistemic stance. In other words, where is belief located when critical inquiry into the material form of the canon takes place? For premodern interpreters, belief precedes understanding, as Anselm's famous *credo ut intelligam* claims. Critical inquiry into the "problems" of the Bible takes place within the context of belief, or faith, on this account, whereas for modern interpreters, belief is necessarily suspended when attending to the "problems" of Scripture for the sake of objectivity and neutrality. This sentiment is illustrated in John Barton's work *The Nature of Biblical Criticism*. He defines one of the constituent trademarks of modern biblical criticism as the "bracketing out" of theological commitments on the front end of one's exegetical inquiry into the Bible.[7]

These matters are of crucial importance when coming to grips with how one actually goes about reading the Old Testament in the light of its human and divine source. The creaturely reality of the Old Testament is affirmed in the Christian tradition. It was written by people who were located in a specific time and place in history, even though identifying their exact temporal location is a challenge we at times cannot overcome, given the present literary shape of the material. The creaturely reality of the Old Testament provides some justification for the spadework that goes into background studies, literary-critical studies, historical analysis, and the host of other matters that fall under the umbrella of exegesis (identifying genitives, wrestling with discourse markers, identifying figures of speech, and so forth). The problem, however, is that Old Testament exegetical work is often reduced to these important nuts and bolts matters. The so-called "meaning" of the text is limited by its creaturely status and historical genesis in a way that the history of Christian reading of the Old Testament finds too hermeneutically limited.

How do governing theological categories such as the primacy of divine

---

6. Neil B. MacDonald, "Illocutionary Stance in Hans Frei's *The Eclipse of Biblical Narrative: An Exercise in Conceptual Redescription and Normative Analysis*," in *After Pentecost: Language and Biblical Interpretation*; ed. C. Bartholomew, C. Greene, and K. Möller (Scripture and Hermeneutics Series 2; Grand Rapids: Zondervan, 2001), 312–28.

7. John Barton, *The Nature of Biblical Criticism* (Louisville: Westminster John Knox, 2007).

authorship govern our understanding of the literary and historical character of the biblical material? Is the creaturely reality of the Bible dealt with
in isolation from other theological commitments? Or is this particular
facet of the Bible's nature governed by other theological commitments?
For example, John Webster allows the doctrine of sanctification to help
situate the Bible's creaturely status in a proper Christian theological framework: God takes ordinary human activities and sets them apart as a unique
means of grace in his divine economy.[8]

Quotes from Brevard Childs and Herman Bavinck will help illustrate
the point. Childs writes, "A corpus of religious writings which has been
transmitted within a community for a thousand years cannot be properly
compared to inert sherds which have lain buried in the ground for centuries."[9] Bavinck gives a more dogmatic account of the matter:

> Scripture, accordingly, does not stand by itself. It may not be construed
> deistically. It is rooted in a centuries-long history and is the fruit of
> God's revelation among the people of Israel and in Christ. Still it is not
> a book of times long past, which only links us with persons and events
> of the past. *Holy Scripture is not an arid story or ancient chronicle but
> the ever-living, eternally youthful Word, which God, now and always,
> issues to his people. It is the eternally ongoing speech of God to us.* It does
> not just serve to give us historical information; it does not even have
> the intent to furnish us a historical story by the standard of reliability
> demanded in other realms of knowledge. Holy Scripture is tendentious:
> whatever was written in former days was written for our instruction,
> that by steadfastness and by the encouragement of the Scriptures we
> might have hope [Romans 15:4]. Scripture was written by the Holy
> Spirit that it might serve him in guiding the church, in the perfecting
> of the saints, in building up the body of Christ. In it God daily comes to
> his people. In it he speaks to his people, not from afar but from nearby
> … It is the living voice of God … Divine inspiration, accordingly, is a
> permanent attribute of Holy Scripture. It was not only "God-breathed"
> at the time it was written; it *is* "God-breathing."[10]

---

8. John Webster, *Holy Scripture: A Dogmatic Sketch* (Current Issues in Theology; Cambridge: Cambridge Univ. Press, 2003), 17–30.

9. Brevard S. Childs, "The Exegetical Significance of Canon for the Study of the Old Testament," in *Congress Volume: Göttingen 1977*, ed. J. A. Emerton, et al. (Supplements to Vetus Testamentum 29; Leiden: Brill, 1978), 78.

10. Herman Bavinck, *Reformed Dogmatics: Prolegomena*, trans. J. Vriend (Grand Rapids: Baker, 2003), 1:384–85, emphasis mine.

These quotations raise a pertinent question: How does our confession about the nature or ontology of the Old Testament as an eternally youthful Word of God determine the way we go about reading it? As T. F. Torrance stated in another context, for a discipline to be "scientific" our methods must be in accord with the nature of the object being studied: the object of study influences, if not determines, the methods used in the study of it.[11] If the Scriptures are, as Christians in the East and the West have always confessed, the living word of God to his people, then our exegetical methods need to be consonant with this confession. What this means, at the end of the day, is that critical tools and methods are a means to an end, not the end in and of themselves. They may help to establish certain aspects of our understanding of the text, but they lack the pneumatic force needed to make the Scriptures be what we confess them to be.

In *Church Dogmatics*, Karl Barth makes the following claim: "Revelation is not a predicate of history, but history is a predicate of revelation."[12] Though Barth is sensitive to the historical genesis of the Old Testament documents, he leans against what he calls "modern theological historicism." This approach presses through the reading of the Bible to reconstructed events outside their literary portrayal and locates revelation in the factuality of the events. Care must be taken here because Barth affirms the historical necessity of the events attested in a historical manner in Scripture — e.g., it is really important that Jesus Christ was raised bodily from the grave; the literary portrayal of this in the gospels is not a mythic depiction of an inner experience of the first-century disciples. He also makes a distinction between historicity and historicality. The former has to do with the factuality of the events attested; the latter has to do with the substance or significance of the event. The Bible, for Barth, assumes historicity but emphasizes historicality. This brings us back to the quote above about the theological relationship between revelation and history. It is revelation that governs our understanding of the significance of the historical events portrayed in the Bible, not history in and of itself.

The text as human production and as divinely inspired are both affirmed on this account. At the same time, the human character of Scripture —

---

11. See Thomas F. Torrance, *Karl Barth: Introduction to Early Theology* (London: SCM Press, 1962), 204; see also his *Karl Barth: Biblical and Evangelical Theologian* (Edinburgh: T&T Clark, 1990), 67 – 68.

12. Karl Barth, *Church Dogmatics*, ed. G. W. Bromiley and T. F. Torrance, trans. G. T. Thomson and Harold Knight (Edinburgh: T&T Clark, 1956), 1:58.

that aspect of Scripture's identity that operates as the driving force behind biblical criticism—is not privatized and sequestered from the particular salvific and revelatory role it plays in the church. The church's confession about the Scripture's inspired status as a written word witnessing to the Living Word in an ongoing dynamic of God's self-presentation governs the way we talk about human authorship and other critical concerns related to its human production. A resistance to literary and historical reconstructions lying behind the text naturally follows from one's confession that the Bible as a written text is the location of God's self-revealing.

This is not to deny the complex nature of the Old Testament's compositional history and the light that such a history may shed on the text being studied. But illustration and illumination differ markedly from substantiation and authentication. The resistance, again, flows from a confession of faith, an article of belief that God has spoken in Jesus Christ and is speaking in Jesus Christ and that the Old and New Testaments are the literary means of this ongoing speaking activity. This confession of faith shapes, if not determines, the way we go about reading the Old Testament as Holy Scripture.

If Christian theology affirms the triune identity of God, which in turn affirms the triune identity of YHWH, then this does indeed change the rule of the interpretive game. Robert Jenson puts the matter bluntly: "If Christ interpreted the old Scripture 'with authority,' as if he were the author, it was because, in the final ontological analysis, that is what he is."[13] If Christian readers of the Bible affirm Jenson's statement—a statement whose substance can be found in the writings of Irenaeus, Luther, and Calvin, just to name a few in the history of interpretation—then our approach to biblical criticism will have to accord with this Christian hermeneutical grammar.

Michael Legaspi ends his helpful *The Death of Scripture and the Rise of Biblical Studies* by claiming that a scriptural Bible and an academic Bible will always be at odds with one another because their respective reading strategies are so radically different.[14] He may be right, though I wonder if the polarity is as evident today in our particular epistemological climate.

---

13. Robert W. Jenson, *Canon and Creed* (Interpretation; Louisville: Westminster John Knox, 2010), 22.

14. Michael C. Legaspi, *The Death of Scripture and the Rise of Biblical Studies* (Oxford Studies in Historical Theology; New York: Oxford Univ. Press, 2010), 169.

Nonetheless, it remains an enduring challenge for Christian readers of the Old Testament to struggle with its creaturely status (and all the matters that pertain to this), while prioritizing the governing role our confession of faith plays in our approach to reading the Bible.

NAME INDEX

SUBJECT INDEX